Yaakov Wodzislawski

My Revenge

Yaakov Wodzislawski

My Revenge

Senior Editors & Producers: Contento De Semrik

Translator: Tanya Rosenblit

Editor: Sharon Gilad

Cover Design: Ivan Bogod

Cover Photo - Sculpture: *A Prisoner in Treblinka Fighting in the Revolt* by Samuel Willenberg

ISBN: 978-9-655-502-053

International sole distributor:
Contento De Semrik
22 Isserles, 67014 Tel-Aviv, Israel
semrik10@gmail.com
www.Semrik.com

Yaakov Wodzislawski

My Revenge

Contento De Semrik

This Book is dedicated

To my beloved parents

And to the millions of Jews

Murdered by the Nazis.

Yaakov "Kuba" Wodzislawski
1925 - 2013

To my beloved Kuba,

I love you, and I will love you

until the end of my days.

Your adoring wife, Irena

ACKNOWLEDGMENTS

I would like to thank my wife, Irena, who has stood by my side throughout our lives in our joint journey towards the future while keeping our commitment to an unbearable past.

Irena, who has worked tirelessly to inform the younger generation:

Pupils, students, soldiers, and anyone who visits our home –

To all of you – my heartfelt thanks.

To our dear friend, Anna Cwiakowska, who contributed greatly and selflessly to the publication of this book, and the translator, Mara Zilberberg, thank you.

Table of Contents

Yaakov Wodzislawski, in the last months of his life, lecturing to visitors
at the Ariel Holocaust and Heroism Memorial House.

Yaakov Wodzislawski (center) and his family in the early 1930s.

The Day I Came Out of the Bunker

Tel Aviv, 1999.

One needs to reflect...

I had just recently left the bunker. Barely 19-years-old, a grown man really, but still...

When I entered the bunker, I was 17.5-years-old, a veteran of four years of Nazi occupation. I was 14-years-old when it all began; I was a high school student. Now I am free, and with this enormous fear that the bunker can be discovered gone, I can no longer chase away the thoughts, not so much about myself and my destiny, but rather about the destiny of my people. It's been going on for such a long time! We are constantly persecuted!

***

...We are constantly persecuted! Since ancient times, from the year 70 B.C. when Titus Caesar ruined the Temple in Jerusalem, forcing the Jews to cease to exist as an independent nation. They were exiled, scattered to the four corners of the world. The persecution of Jews has continued from then on. Despite the relatively good financial conditions they were able to create in their new communities, they did not have personal freedom. Denounced and scorned, despised and disgraced, they were often gathered in overcrowded ghettoes.

Afterward, Spain: persecutions, torture and finally expulsion—the massive dispersion of Jews, who formed new communities in other European countries, which while facilitating the birth of important ideals, also brought with it a new tidal wave of anti-Semitism and hatred.

Anti-Semitism has been prevalent since the early days of history, from the moment the Jews found themselves in exile. During the Middle Ages, they were forced to wear a mark of shame in the form of a yellow badge or a circle on their outerwear, as well as ridiculous pointy hats. The ghetto was nearly the only place of residence for Jews and they were not allowed to live outside of it.

Time did not bring any significant improvement for the Jewish issue—on the contrary: what was once bad had gotten even worse.

A short time before World War I, anti-Semitism grew so strong that the Jews realized something had to be done to resolve the issue. They had hoped to do so by establishing their own national state, their own homeland.

World War I broke out on July 28, 1914 and Europe's valleys overflowed with blood. Among the victims were the Jews that were murdered in the pogroms in the Ukraine.

In Russia, the days following the fall of the Tsarist regime were a time of chaos and internal strife. Simon Petlura and Nestor Makhno, who were both sworn enemies of the Jews, led the Ukraine. Wherever Petlura and Makhno's loyalists went, Jews were mercilessly slaughtered. Those who survived the war fell to the swords, knives, and bullets of the Ukrainian killers. And why? Because they were Jews...

The world remained unfazed. No one defended these wretched souls and no one was concerned by the mass murder of innocent people. For who could have defended them? Did Jews have rights as a people back then? Jews everywhere raised their voices in protest, as a national minority, but no one cared about them.

In March 1918, a general peace treaty was signed— U.S. President Woodrow Wilson's famous "Fourteen Points" plan. Together with other treaties signed to bring about the end of the war, these agreements considered various peoples as eligible for their own national homes—only the Jews were left out.

There were many discussions about equal rights for all minorities, including the Jews, but as the future soon proved, equality did not exist in reality.

In the meantime, the Zionist Movement was growing strong.

After the Kishinev Pogrom of 1903, Jews realized that a practical solution for the Jewish issue had to be devised. The youth were the first to understand that a people longing for appreciation and respect must have a homeland of its own that would safeguard its national affairs.

After World War I, everything went "back to normal" and the previous anti-Jewish riots soon resumed. On the pretext of economic crises, Jews were fought against on all fronts. Anti-Semites started to defame and castigate Jews worldwide and different organizations were created to fight the Jews, not only with words, but also with terrorist activities. It grew particularly strong when Adolf Hitler appeared on the scene with his racist theories, in the early 1920s.

Anti-Semites now had a new battlefield to fight on: a new doctrine joined the economic struggle against the Jews—scientific racism.

When the Nazis came to power in 1933, their first order of business was to dispossess the Jews of all political, economic, and cultural positions, but this was merely the prelude of the Nazis' objective: A time of massive arrests and deportations to concentration camps had arrived, and Jews were no longer safe. Be it day or night, SS and Gestapo shock troops implemented the most sophisticated methods to harass innocent people just for being Jews.

Refugees from Germany were stranded at sea for months on end because no country would accept them until they fell victims to the Nazi killers.

Meanwhile, the Polish town of Zbąszyń, on the German-Polish border, experienced dramatic events: The Germans deported German Jews, who were former

Polish citizens, back to Poland, but the latter denied them entry. Only international pressure eventually led to Poland's yielding.

After Hitler entered Austria and Czechoslovakia in 1938, the Jews in those countries suffered the same fate as the German Jews. There were those that committed suicide with their entire families to avoid falling into the hands of the Nazi murderers.

On September 1, 1939, Hitler conquered Poland. World War II, in which Jewish victims were the largest in number, had begun. History had not yet seen such things as those inflicted on us by the Germans. No nation has ever had to endure such a Holocaust, such humiliation, torture and suffering; no nation has ever had to sacrifice so many lives. Since ancient times, no people have ever gone through such horrors, meant to bring about their destruction, as the Jewish people have.

For the first time in the history of the world, death factories were created, factories that employed innovative technology focused on human extermination on an industrial scale. Death camps were established with the primary goal of slowly exterminating people in favor of the German nation, but only after extracting the last bit of strength that they had in them. Hitler's first mission, in all of the countries he conquered, was the extermination of the Jews. The final annihilation of the Jewish population was done via mass murders in all countries almost simultaneously; and the blood of murdered men, women and children, young and old, was flowing. Jews were shuttled to Poland from all over Europe by train, to fertilize the land with their ashes. Entire worlds of people who had so much to contribute in every field were gone. They were Jews, so for them, there was no pardon, not one ounce of mercy.

In these inhumane conditions, the isolated and forsaken Jewish youth rose up in an armed struggle against the Germans. No one dared to dream of victory and each of them knew they would be fighting to their death. And fall in battle they did. The Warsaw ghetto warriors, who fought the armed German forces for three weeks, demonstrated how Jews could mount a fight faced with indescribable circumstances. Almost everyone who participated in this brave uprising was killed, but their deaths were shrouded in glory.

The world looked at the Jews differently.

In addition to fighting in the ghettoes, Jews also fought in the forests. Their enemies were often not only the Germans, but also the local fascists, who were thirsty for Jewish blood. The Jews also joined the regular armies, fighting against the Germans on all fronts. Jewish fighters also participated in the Polish revolt in Warsaw in August 1944. In May 1945, Nazi Germany was forced to sign a treaty of unconditional surrender. Germany had lost the war.

Those who survived the war left the concentration camps. They were miserable, indigent, liberated human wrecks with no roof over their heads and no family or friends to turn to. They were starting a new life in freedom, but their future was not bright at all. There was peace in Europe, but while it seemed that after so much death and suffering—and especially given Germany's surrender—anti-Semitism would cease to exist, but that was not the case. Anti-Semitism was alive and well and surprisingly, not only was it was undiminished by the war—it was growing stronger.

Pogroms against Jews took place in Odessa, in the Soviet Union, and in Poland as well. The Poles witnessed the murders the Germans had committed against the Jews on Polish soil; and now, with a meager number of Jews left in the country—survivors who were searching for what was left of their former homes—the Poles unleashed pogroms against them. Such was the case in the city of Kielce, where cold arms in Krakow and in other places murdered more than 40 Jews.

The world saw how the Germans renounced their responsibility for the murder of six million Jews in Europe. They did not answer for that, and were not made to assume any blame. That is why anti-Semitism continues to rear its head.

The Jews who survived the war had no sense of security. Their existence seemed temporary and their future was neither clear nor safe. But there was one path that called to all of them: the road to Palestine—the only salvation against the next mass annihilation of the Jews. The concentration of multitudes of Jews, as many as possible, came to the Land of Israel to form a strong and robust Jewish national home; a homeland with an army to defend the Jews that remained in the Diaspora—that hope would be their salvation.

We are aware of the many difficulties, but through perseverance and sacrifice, we will reach what is for us a matter of our very survival. We believe that our efforts will not be in vain. The memory of the six million Jews brutally annihilated will be our incentive. They demand it of us. This is our revenge!

—Written in Poland, 1945.

My Childhood in Poland

My name is Yaakov "Kova" Wodzislawski. I was born in the city of Częstochowa, Poland, in 1925. My father, Shmuel, son of Sara and Zeev, and my mother, Rosa, daughter of Zeev and Dora Tenzer, had three sons; my eldest brother, Zeev, was born in 1921, my brother, Yehiel "Heniek," was born in 1923, and I was the youngest.

Father was a wholesale trader. He bought merchandise in Warsaw and sold it to shopkeepers in the city. Mother was a homemaker and raised the children. We were not a wealthy family, but we wanted for nothing. We lived in a mixed neighborhood of Poles and Jews, and we had good relations with our neighbors.

My parents wanted a better future for their children and they made sure we studied and acquired a higher education so we would not become merchants. There were many books in the house and reading was our main pastime.

At the age of six, I started studying at the national school that was meant only for Jewish children. We studied for seven hours a day, Monday to Friday, but Judaism studies were not the main focus.

After I graduated from elementary school, I went to the gymnasium (secondary school). This school was considered as one of the best schools in all of Poland. Each school had an ID number. The school I went to was No. 326. The number was embroidered on the uniform jacket and since the school was known for its achievements, its graduates could get into any university in Poland without admission tests. It was a great honor to study in that school.

In 1935, my big brother Zeev, who was 14 years old and a junior in high school at the time, became sick with cancer and died. Everyone in town heard of the tragedy that befell my family and the high school headmaster, Podolsky, who was a celebrity in Poland, came to the funeral.

I entered high school on September 1, 1938. I was the only Jewish student in class. I didn't tell anyone about my being Jewish at first, but the teachers knew and therefore exempted me from religion classes. After my peers noticed my absence from these classes and started asking questions, I told them I was Jewish. After that, their attitude toward me changed—anti-Semitism was already present in the hearts of the nation at that time.

Even before the war broke out we knew that Poland was heading for difficult days, especially for the Jews. News of what was happening in Germany and the restrictive laws the Jews were facing there had reached us, as well. We knew that the day when we would suffer the same was not far. We were mentally prepared for that, but we underestimated the Germans' monstrosity.

Sometime before the war, after the Molotov-Ribbentrop Pact was signed in August 1939, my mother sent my uncle and me to the city of Kielce, which was farther away from the German border. The war broke out on Friday, September 1, 1939. I remember listening to the radio and hearing a volley of messages from the Polish government and army. The city was not under attack yet, and I heard testimonies of many refugees who flocked to the city. I also heard that my birth city of Częstochowa was bombed and destroyed. I was scared, helpless, and worried about the future of my family. After a few days, German planes started to bomb Kielce. I was lucky: I hid inside a house and after I left it and moved to another hiding place, I saw that it had been bombed, razed to the ground.

After a few days, I woke up in the early hours of the morning and went outside to buy some bread. I stood in line at the bakery and not far from me stood a Jewish boy in traditional clothing. Suddenly, I heard the sound of engines. A few minutes later German soldiers on motorcycles approached us. Poles stood on both sides of the street, many of them were crying. A girl came out of the group of Poles that was closest to me, stopped one of the soldiers, pointed to the Jewish lad and said, "Yid!" repeating it several times. Luckily, the soldier looked at him and moved on.

At that moment I thought, *What a fink!* This was

such a tragic time for the Poles as well, and the only thing she could think to do was to rat out this poor soul, who was left standing pale and shaking with fear. It was interesting to see how no one in that group of women tried to stop her or said anything.

After about a week, I went back to Częstochowa. The Germans had re-opened the schools, but not for Jews. Since I was going to a non-Jewish institution, I went back to school, but a few days later, we were expelled from it in disgrace. We would sit, my brother Heniek and me, at home reading books.

I remember an incident that happened a few months after the war began: We had a bicycle at home. One day, a German in uniform came to our house, accompanied by a Pole. They entered the apartment and took the bicycle even though I had a permit from the Germans to have it—a permit I obtained through a German class-mate.

By the end of 1939, the Jews in Częstochowa were made to wear a white band with a blue Star of David on their clothes. The Poles could identify the Jews without the band, but it made our foreignness that much more obvious.

Father had savings, mainly in dollars and not in Polish zloty. This money helped us survive for a while and we managed to buy food from the Poles until we had to move to the ghetto.

The First German Shots Toward Civilian Population

On a sunny Sunday, September 3, 1939, the first German units entered Częstochowa. The armies of the chosen nation marched with an arrogant stride, the German soldiers bursting with pride and joy.

Tanks and armored cars were driving along the city streets one after another and long lines of trucks were moving to the east. Supply convoys, some loaded on horseback, but mostly on vehicles, would occasionally stop to rest. Huge gun barrels peeped through the protective sheets, their murderous mouths gaping at the audience. Airplane squadrons were flying in close formations over the city in a victorious display, as the enormous German war mechanism flowed through the veins of the city.

From the moment the German armies entered, the city became relatively quiet. It seemed as if the soldiers and officers treated the civilian population with respect. When the initial fear subsided, the residents came out into the streets to behold the conquerors, to see the armies that were going to become rulers of the land. People seemed somewhat surprised: Polish propaganda described the Germans as monsters, and they turned out to be people who were respectful of another nation's rights.

Disappointment, shock, and disillusionment came soon enough. The illusion of tranquility lasted barely two days. The faux silence turned out to be the preface to the population's murder. The Germans removed their polite mask of hypocrisy and their true colors were revealed.

At noon, without reason or warning, soldiers throughout the city, armed with automatic weapons, started firing in all directions. The residents, who did not expect such a thing, had no time to hide when the murderous bullets started whistling through the air, and soon the streets were awash with blood. The first civilian victims fell to the ground. The image was horrifying. People ran through the streets, hopelessly trying to save themselves. Every now and then, you could see a man or a woman running toward the gate of a house in an attempt to seek shelter, only to fall prey to a bullet. All doubt was gone and a terrible understanding set in: this was what life was going to be like under the Nazi occupation.

A few hours later, the shooting stopped. Now it was time for the killer Nazi's magnificently staged "aktzia": Residents thrown out into the streets were ordered to assemble in all of the big public buildings, churches, and plazas. Everyone was deported with no thought to their age, marital status, or nationality, the old and the young, priests, and monks, Jews and Poles. This great crowd was ordered to walk with their hands raised and their heads down in fear. Their horrified faces were as pale as those of the dead.

After the crowds were assembled at the collection points, people were ordered to lie on the ground. The Germans said that anyone who raises his head would be shot. Machine guns were placed around the crowd and when the sign was given, the soldiers started shooting over people's heads. The bullets were flying low, and anyone who carelessly lifted his head, did not live to see the light of day. The suffering was immense: to lie in an uncomfortable position for several hours, with gunfire constantly threatening from above. Sounds of crying and nervous sobs were heard sporadically. Prayers were said out loud. People were saying goodbye to each other and no one held any hope to survive this trap. The most heart-wrenching sight was that of the little children, who did not understand what was going on.

The "game" continued for hours. No one was hungry—no one could think of food. The thirst, on the other hand, was grueling. Throats were dry, but no one dared ask for some water. The air was ripe with stench, since worse than the thirst was the feculence of bodily functions. But no one noticed. Everyone's nerves were strained to the limit. Do not raise your head... Anyone who was betrayed by his nerves fell to a German bullet. As time passed, the number of those that fell multiplied and the ground was covered in red puddles.

As evening approached, the glare of fire appeared in the sky. It could be seen in every part of the city, dim at first, but it became stronger as the flames spread. The sight was horrifying: red color ruled the sky and red ruled the earth, too. The army surrounded the houses set on fire by the Germans and the residents were not allowed to leave them. Those who ran were shot to death and those who were not killed by bullets were burned to death in their homes. Only a few managed to slip through the German blockade.

Nightfall ended the death game. All those who were crammed into the plazas, lying with their faces to the ground, were ordered to stand up. Not everyone did. Shrunken characters continued lying on the ground here and there. People passed them by, shaking, as the Germans—who were in a very good mood—made derogatory remarks, filled with contempt and laughter, kicking the dead bodies as they passed them. A procession that looked like a ghost march was formed. Everyone was walking with their hands held high in the air, their faces pale. Many had nervous tremors, a result of what they had gone through, and fear of what was yet to come. Soldiers that were armed from head to toe, pointing their guns at people, surrounded the procession. Single shots could be heard every now and then, but they soon died as well.

The fires grow brighter, meanwhile, spreading from the burning houses to neighboring homes. Blood-red flashes reflected off the faces of passersby. Some of them burst into tears when they went by the home of their relatives or friends. The entire procession was led to the prison and its cells filled up quickly. The prison cells were so crowded that no one could sit or lie down. When the prison was full, people were locked in its cells, its basements, and the stables, in similar conditions to those who were in jail. Everyone was left standing, crammed inside the cells, plagued by constant thirst that was made worse by the heat in the crowded cells.

The night passed in an atmosphere of uncertainty. The cells were silent, no one said a word, and everyone was preoccupied with their own anxieties. No one had any illusions. At this point, it was obvious that the Germans would not be deterred from committing any crime.

The morning brought no improvement, just the opposite—the lack of air and the stench were becoming unbearable and the lack of water was the hardest to deal with. People were losing their ability to cope with the conditions and some fainted, but no one had the courage to ask for water. Necessity eventually prevailed; for soon everyone would faint and no one would be able to scream for help, so the bravest ones started pounding on the door: "Water! Water!"

No one answered for a long time, but then the door opened and a soldier wearing a helmet stood at the entrance, his gun pointed at the people in the cell. A diabolic smile spread across his face at the sight of the tortured and humiliated people. When he saw what was going on inside the cell, he blurted something to his comrade. After a moment, everyone was hosed down with water. Everyone lunged at the puddles that remained on the floor, crawling and pushing—drinking the filthy, disgusting liquid was all that mattered. Some rubbed water on the faces of those who fainted, to resuscitate them.

A depressing atmosphere spread inside the cell. People were whispering to one another, some prayed to God and a soft cry could be heard here and there, one from a young man who could not contain himself. The greatest congestion was felt near the window that allowed a little air to come in from the dirty yard. The strong took their place near the bars; the weak got the least air. The hours were growing infinitely long and every minute seemed like an eternity. The hands on the clock moved slowly, as if on purpose. This went on until the afternoon hours, when the doors to all the cells opened and the order "Out!" was heard. Everyone gathered in the prison yard, surrounded by a stifling chain of SS and army men. After a few moments, several officers appeared. They chose the youngest and the oldest from the crowd and released them. The rest were taken back to the cells.

The city was in an appalling state. Torched houses were still burning and bodies were lying in the streets. Reinforced military patrols were roaming the streets and machine guns were placed on street corners. The emptiness was everywhere and no one dared to step out into the abandoned streets. In several public gardens, where defense trenches had been dug, people were burying the victims of the previous day.

An announcement was published in the afternoon ordering all the residents who remained in their homes to leave them, clear the churches, and gather in the public service buildings and the plaza, in order to enable two Germans to conduct a search for weapons. The Germans claimed that the civilian population had weapons, which they allegedly used to shoot German soldiers. That was the reason for the retaliation. And once more the same "game" had begun, and once again there were victims. The Germans passed through several streets, searching one house after another. They found nothing until—lo and behold! A German officer stepped out of one of the houses holding a long object that did not resemble a weapon at all. It turned out to be a shaving machine and razor blades, deemed as a weapon and whose possession was now barred.

The second day of hell had ended. The glow from the fires could still be seen in the sky—the German soldiers set a few more buildings on fire to make a statement. The residents were released to their homes. The young and those who appeared healthy were arrested and taken to the prison where their families brought them food, because the Germans gave them nothing. The fate of those who were arrested remains unknown.

After a few days, the door was opened again and everyone was taken out to the same yard. Now the

Germans selected the sick, the weak and the Jews—who they intended to "handle" separately—the gates were opened and people were released without the escort of guns. But those who remained behind were doomed, for they were about to be taken to forced labor camps in Germany.

***

The city could not shake off the nightmare of those days of fear and murder, claiming 1,200 innocent lives fallen to Nazi bullets. Many of those that were persecuted became sick. Many of the wounded died in the hospitals. During the first days of the war, the households that had lost their loved ones were in mourning. Those were the first victims of the Nazi crimes in Poland.

The Belzec and Cieszanów Camps

It was the latter half of 1940. The Germans ordered the Jewish Council, the *Judenrat*, to supply them with people for a paying work camp. It was not an easy thing to do, as the Jews had completely lost their faith in the Germans and they no longer believed their promises. The Jewish Council was faced with a difficult dilemma because if they failed to meet the demand for a work-force, Judenrat officials would be made to go in their place and they and their families would pay with their lives.

The council had to choose young and healthy people. The Germans did not care who was chosen as long as they were young, more or less able-bodied and that they met the quotas. The council started campaigning: those who will go to the work camps, they promised, will enjoy better living conditions, no food shortage and be free of harassment and belligerence.

The Jews were in a dire economic state. Food was scarce and no one could get minimal wages to cover basic domestic needs, yet prices were rising every day. Many families starved and others were living in extremely difficult conditions. The Jewish Council chose those people for their assignment, promising them they could send home the money they will earn.

I learned the history of those days from my brother Heniek, who survived those ordeals:

The day when young people lined up on the street had arrived. They carried a backpack or a parcel on their shoulders and were accompanied by their families. The mothers offered advice and final instructions and then it was time to say goodbye: There were tears and handshakes; feeble smiles on the faces of those youth. They had no premonition of what lay ahead. They disappeared inside the building and their mothers were left standing there, looking at the gate, their expressions showing what they felt: pain and despair.

In the hall of the old factory, the atmosphere was pretty light, as it usually is with youth. There was singing, loud chatting, someone was playing the harmonica, and another was talking to his audience. But the doubts were often raised as to whether all the promises the Judenrat had made were going to be fulfilled. People's faces were turning grim, but there was no turning back. The military policemen by the gate did not let anyone leave.

Every now and then new people came in, and the hall was slowly filling up. There was a rumor that the entire "shipment" was supposed to leave the next day and it turned out to be true. The next day, in the pouring rain, a line of Jews left toward the train station, densely surrounded by armed military policemen. On the sides of the road, relatives and acquaintances escorted them, but the Germans did not let anyone come close. They could only give them one last look from afar, one last hand gesture of goodbye.

Once at the train station, the passengers were given supplies for the road—not from the Germans, but from the Jewish Council. No one knew where he or she was going, and no one spoke of it. Everyone waited for the train to arrive. Some of them were impatient, but how do you escape the hands of the military police?

Finally, the locomotive and cars arrived, and on sight of them, all doubts were gone. They were cattle cars, each with one window barred with a wire. It was clear that what these young people were facing was not safe. There was a feeling that something bad was going to happen. The Germans slated 80 people for each car, cramming them inside it. The cars were sealed and uniformed men, probably the SS, escorted the train. The train started to move toward the evening hours and a Yiddish melody sounded from the cars, "Brothers, brothers, home, home..."

A candle was lit inside the car, everyone gathered around it, seated on his or her backpacks. No one thought of sleeping, there was not enough room. A general sense of depression ruled, growing stronger the farther the train moved, away from where home and relatives were left. The night passed with uncertainty and trepidation about what tomorrow would bring.

The train was eastbound, stopping in nearly every

station. At noon, it stopped for the last time. Have we reached our destination? No one knew. The seals were broken and the doors were open, revealing a train station with many uniformed men. From that moment on, everything happened very quickly. An order to disembark the cars was given, accompanied by the lashing of whips and beatings with the butts of rifles. It was an ominous welcome, but there was no time to ponder over it. They had to get in line as quickly as possible and a thick ring of SS soldiers surrounded it. On the streets of Lublin, where the line marched, many military men could be seen, but only few civilians and the Jews were not seen at all. The city looked like a military base. The line progressed quickly, hastened by the soldiers' shouts and punches.

After a while, the camp was revealed, well fenced with several lines of barbed wire. There were guard towers with machine guns and powerful spotlights in the corners. Inside the fenced area lines of sheds could be seen.

The new "recruits" were brought into this camp, which was called Lipowa. Everyone was ordered to obey the strict discipline that was administered there. The penalty for every offense, the newcomers were told, was death—which was prevalent here.

After eating something turbid that was supposed to be lunch, the people, tired from the ride, went to sleep. But their sleep was constantly interrupted. The guards were practicing shooting for fun, and at times, someone would actually get shot. Oh well—what's one less Jew in the world?

The camp was strongly lit at night: The posts were reinforced and an SS soldier armed with an automatic weapon stood on the roof of every shed. Those who tried to escape could get out alive only by the grace of a miracle. And with 300-400 people crammed into each shed, the stench was suffocating.

The next day, the passengers were ordered to prepare for another leg of the journey. Inside the car, everyone was discussing the events of the last few days. People understood what their lives were going to look like under the "protection" of the SS.

After several hours, the train stopped at a tiny station. The process of having people debark the cars was repeated, only this time with much less consideration and greater cruelty. It was Belzec, a small town on the Soviet border. The population was mostly Ukrainian and there were no Jews there at all. Those that had the chance crossed over to the Soviet side. There was a work camp in the area that was meant for Jews and Gypsies.

The newcomers saw razed buildings, barracks, and stables all without rooftops, windows, or doors. Fires were lit everywhere at night, around them were Gypsies in worn-out clothes, women in torn skirts and half-naked children.

The Jews who were already there told the newcomers about the horrible conditions. This is a place where people were disposed of, they said. The Jews in Belzec were treated worse than animals. Apart from the bad food, the poor living conditions, the hard work and the beatings, the threat of a death sentence was constant—and not only for an offense, but also just for the guards' amusement, to fulfill their murderous desires. The sanitary conditions were appalling. Swarms of lice and parasites of all sizes infested the buildings and straw mats, burrowing into the people's clothing. Fighting them was impossible, because without the proper sanitary conditions killing them was useless. They even swam in the coffee, so no one drank it.

The nights were even harder: the lice stung, and the stench everywhere was stifling. The SS soldiers fired their weapons to pass the time and it was possible to hear stray bullets hitting the wall. This pastime claimed many lives. The wounded did not survive. Whoever was injured was killed on the spot and the same went for the sick. An outbreak of dysentery plagued the camp and could not be contained, as there were no medicines.

In the morning, an order was given to continue. People were made to march 30 kilometers on foot, under the burning morning sun, from Belzec to Cieszanów, where they had to build a new camp. The line was flanked by SS soldiers on bicycles and a cart carrying a machine gun ready for action was at its back. Anyone who walked this road and survived will never forget it for the rest of his life.

The SS soldiers began expediting the line as soon as the march started, demanding that people walk faster.

Those who were unable to do so felt a whip at their back. The heat became heavy and with it, so did the SS soldiers' prodding. The strong ones somehow managed to go forward; the weak ones were left behind and beaten mercilessly. People threw their belongings away to make their march easier. Everyone was sweating and their breathing became short, but their tormentors had no mercy. Suddenly, gunshots were heard. An older man who could not walk at the required pace was shot. Everyone understood that they only had to give their escorts the slightest reason and they would meet the same fate.

The road was littered with the parcels people had dropped, but no one stopped to notice. Everyone tried to avoid the beatings that were constantly and ruthlessly handed out. The thirst was tormenting, but the SS soldiers did not allow anyone to stop and drink water. They, themselves extravagantly drank beer with undisguised pleasure.

Someone passed out. His friends wanted to save him, but the lashing of whips and beatings from the butts of rifles hit anyone who came close. Suddenly the rattling of the machine gun sounded and the misery of the man who lay on the ground was over. The line kept on walking. More and more people stayed behind and more and more gun shots were heard. A few medics from Częstochowa approached the military escort's commander and asked him to allow them to put the parcels carried by the weak on the cart, to help them through the march. After many requests, the commander granted their wish. No more shots were heard after that. Only the medics could be seen, helping the weak, who were barely moving their legs along.

The journey reached its end with an enormous effort by the marchers, who needed every remaining ounce of strength to complete it. After a while, the little Ukrainian town that was the purpose of this "journey" could be seen. Not everyone arrived. A few older men, those that were taken from the camp in Belzec and were exhausted after several months there, fell on the way.

The place where the Cieszanów camp was about to be built had buildings that served as a synagogue, a mikveh and a Jewish school, as well as a few other buildings that remained intact after the Jews had left. The buildings had no roof, doors, or windows and the locals dismantled the floors long ago to use the wood for heating. The only water well was behind a fenced area. Every few hours the well would empty because the entire camp, over 3,000 people, drew water from it. Tired from the journey, the people lay down to sleep on the ground.

The SS, headed by Major Dolf, one of the organizers of Dachau, were responsible for overseeing the camp. With time, it turned out that Dolf, a short and heavy middle-aged man who was always accompanied by a giant sheep dog, was a barbaric sadist who knew no limits. Soon, the entire camp dreaded him. When the words "I'm leaving" sounded, everyone became silent with fear, for it was known that after his departure he always left a few corpses and several tortured people.

The Germans ordered the people to form a Jewish *lagerrat* (camp council), which was tasked with organizing life in the compound: to build a kitchen, a clinic, and a mailroom, and to introduce some order in general. This council also included police officers who were responsible for instilling public order. A dysentery plague soon broke out and everyone fell sick. There were no medicines, but the Germans did not release anyone from work. Nutrition in the camp consisted of black coffee and 120 grams of black bread that was baked from a mixture of fibers and flour. For "lunch," they had soup that contained a little murky water and several pieces of unpeeled potatoes. There was no oil or meat. No one had anything for dinner.

The sanitary conditions were unbearable. The straw "mattresses" on which people slept were infested with lice. No one changed their underwear, because no one could wash their clothes for lack of water. The clothes were weathered and with time, people were walking around in rags. It was hard to bathe because there was only one well, which was outside the camp. There were a few cases when the prisoners were shot as they were drawing water. The SS soldiers claimed that the Jews were shot during an attempted escape.

The purpose of the work was digging and fortifying the anti-tank trenches on the Soviet-German border. Certain work stations reached several meters from the border fence. The work was conducted in two shifts, supervised by the SS. No rest was allowed. If anyone so much as lifted their shovel slowly, an SS soldier would immediately approach them, pull them from the trench and beat them with the butt of his rifle. The medics had their hands full. From the first moment, the Germans showed the Jews no mercy. Very early in the morning the camp's residents were ordered to form lines and walk to the worksite, which was several kilometers away from the camp. The Jewish workers went through the town with their shovels on their shoulders and their heads lowered. They were accompanied by armed SS soldiers with whips in their hands. Everyone was ordered to march according to a pace the military dictated. Any misstep was met with the crack of the whip or the butt of a gun.

The worst part was crossing a small stream with a rickety bridge hanging over it. Young people went across the obstacle easily, but the older ones found it difficult. The first rows crossed over just fine, but disorder ruled the next ones and several elderly people barely crossed the bridge. The SS soldiers expected it: they were standing by the bridge, beating whoever failed to cross the bridge fast enough for them. Those that failed were pushed into the water and were ordered to walk in wet clothes. After that, the Germans ordered them to sing loudly. If the order was not fulfilled quickly enough, the Germans would become enraged, beating people and shooting in all directions. And so, singing, the lines would come to work.

Hectic work followed, shovels cutting through the air and throwing the ground. Suddenly, one of the SS soldiers decided one of the Jews was working too slowly. In a fit of rage he grabbed the man's shovel and started beating him over the head with it. The victim started bleeding, which only provoked his attacker even more. He cocked his weapon and killed the man.

And so the work went on.

Freedom was so close! The barbed wires on the border, which could be passed easily, were so close! And there, one could take a full and free breath of air! They could see how on the other side of the border Red Army soldiers were walking by, how life was tranquil and quiet over there. The yearning to run away from this hell, from this grave, while we are still alive, broke our hearts.

These fractured thoughts were interrupted by shouting. A German had found a few potatoes in one of the backpacks. He beat the owner of the backpack and kicked him mercilessly. Afterward, he ordered two men to lift the man off the ground, take him and throw him into the excrement hole. The workers refused the order, so the Nazi grabbed the victim himself and threw him into the hole, where he eventually died. The two men who refused the order received 25 flogs each.

One "event" followed another and then the workday was over. The Jews returned to the camp, where another hell awaited. The elderly, exhausted from a day of labor, were barely able to cross the broken bridge, the Nazis pounding them. And again, they marched through the town's streets. It was Sunday, and all around them people were dressed in their best clothes, walking in groups. I asked myself, will I see my home and my family, too, one day?

Those that returned to camp, learned that a manhunt was conducted for those that did not report for work. Dolf led the chase himself. A thorough search was conducted in all of the buildings and three exhausted, sick people, who were unable to walk, were found. Dolf, mad with fury, started beating them with a heavy wooden rod. They now lay dying in their own blood. The SS soldiers refrained awhile from shooting them so that those who were returning from work were forewarned of the punishment imposed on those who did not want to work.

It was autumn and the night came on quickly. The people, exhausted, were already asleep. Suddenly, at midnight, gunshots were heard. The drunken SS soldiers came back from a feast and they were now amusing themselves. Bullets were whistling closeby, especially near the clinic's ambulance. People had to cling to the ground to escape the danger. Everything calmed down after several hours, but in the morning, it turned out that two people were shot and several others were wounded.

Nothing in the camp could be repaired. Letters from home would arrive now and then, giving the prisoners a little solace. One day, after work, everybody heard that one of the SS soldiers had dragged a Jew to the observation tower and threw him off it. It turned out that the guard was upset that he did not get his lunch on time and that was his way of venting his anger. His victim died several hours later.

People, in their initial desperation, were still trying to devise ways to escape, but those illusions soon dissipated. Two managed to sneak through the fence and cross over to the Soviet side, but the Russians ordered them to turn back. Their report about what was happening to the Jews in the camp was met with nothing but shrugs. Only few managed to escape, the rest were caught and incarcerated in the Lublin dungeons.

One night, a man from the Częstochowa group was shot. He went out to relieve himself and a shot sounded. A moment later, dozens of shots rang through the entire camp. The man returned wounded and bleeding and everyone woke up. Gunshots and German shouts came through the windows. SS soldiers appeared in the room, flashlights in hand, demanding to know where the injured man was. No one answered; everyone understood why they were looking after him. The enraged Germans started searching. Friends tried to hide the injured man, but a trail of blood gave away his location. He was ordered to step outside, but he resisted, begging them to spare his life. The man was pleading with heartbreaking cries: "Brothers, help! I am young! I want to live! I am an only child, the only provider for my family! My mother will not be able to bare it!" But how could anyone help him with the Germans' guns pointing at them? The entire room was crying helplessly.

A moment later, he was shot to death.

No one slept that night, the sight they witnessed was etched in their memory. No one said anything; everyone understood each other without words. The moment was unifying, giving everyone a shared goal—to survive and seek vengeance.

The SS soldier who killed the man from Częstochowa reported the incident to his commander saying, "Ich habe einen hund erschossen" (I shot a dog), to which the camp's commander answered, "Du hast einen tag frei" (you have a day off).

Once Częstochowa learned of the terrible news from letters sent by those who went away, somber despair clouded everyone. Families who had a relative in the camp, lived in constant anxiety. A letter that arrived to one of families said, "Dear parents! No pen could describe what takes place here. I have only one request of you: sell my best clothes and whatever else you can spare and send me money and food, for what good will those things do me if I don't survive this horrible camp?"

After the news was out, Częstochowa's Jews became very anxious. There were those that followed their relatives in an attempt to locate the camp and see it for themselves. Maybe there, in that place, something could be done. People risked their lives to help those closest to them. The families spared no effort or money, but the fact was that nothing could be done.

With time, the work in Cieszanów was nearly over. The anti-tank trenches that the Jews dug stretched across many kilometers. Every inch of soil was soaked with blood and tears. Now they were all thinking about one thing: Will the Nazis release them to their homes or will they have to endure more torture at a different camp?

After eight weeks at the Cieszanów camp, an order was given that everyone, except for the *lagerrat* (camp council), had to line up in the plaza. Hopeful, people quickly complied and within minutes, they were outside the camp's gate. Now, the walk to Belzec began. Despite their fatigue, people marched quickly with the sole purpose of getting as far away from the hellish fences as possible.

After a night in Belzec, the cars made their way back. Everyone wanted to get home as quickly as possible, to be with the people closest to them and as far away as possible from those bad days and nights. After a few days stay at Radom, where they had a warm welcome from the Jewish community, the slave labor workers continued on their way to Częstochowa.

And again, not everyone was fortunate. Some were cunningly removed from the group and sent to one of the camps in the area.

There were several camps named Belzec.

In a publication released in 1946 in the city of Lodge by the Jewish Central Historical Society, titled

"Documents and Materials: Camps—Volume 1," Magistrate N. Blumental writes:

On August 14, 1940, following their dispatch to labor, 10,000 Jews went through Belzec, from almost the entire region of the Generalgouvernement. This camp became a center that contained nine points: Belzec—the yard, Belzec—the flourmill, Belzec—the locomotive station, Cieszanów, Lipsko, and Plaszow.

In the autumn of 1941, the construction of a concentration camp in Belzec began.

The labor camp described here was built in Cieszanów in the first half of 1940, and was part of Belzec. In the autumn of 1941, the construction of a death camp in Belzec began.

Life in the Ghetto

It was the spring of 1941. The first breezes brought with them to Częstochowa news of how the German were sending Jews to the ghettoes. It was no longer enough for the Germans that the Jews were made to wear yellow stars on their clothes. They decided to assemble them within the narrow boundaries of a ghetto. The rumors turned out to be true. Here too, the Germans acted with their trademark precision.

In April, a decree had come ordering Jews to leave their homes and move to a special area, earmarked just for them, away from the non-Jewish population. The order stipulated that if after a set date, anyone was found in the Aryan side, they would be shot.

The move to the ghetto took place on Passover, of all days. Wagons loaded with personal possessions of all kinds labored across the city. Those who could not afford to pay for a proper cargo wagon dragged small carts. The streets were crowded with traffic and action, making the move all that harder.

The Jewish property looked meager and poor: all the good furniture, linens, paintings, rugs, utensils, chandeliers and anything that had any value had long been plundered by the Gestapo, the *Schutzstaffel* (SS), the military police and other Nazi mobs. Possessions that a family worked for and accumulated, sometimes over decades, property of financial and sentimental value, collections that took years to assemble, were all gone within minutes. But no one cared, or dared to complain either. Material losses were of no great concern in times of persecution and murder.

For the Jews, it was the beginning of a new time of living in the ghetto, in exigency and squalor; cordoned off, with no ability to get out.

The Judenrat—the Jewish Council—played a key role during this move. The Germans, to make it easier for themselves, created a Jewish administration that had to meet the orders issued by the Gestapo or the *Stadthauptman* (the city mayor) and, at times, by low-ranking Nazi officers. Accordingly, the Jewish Council supervised the deportation operation of 1941.The Judenrat would come to play a very important role in the lives of the Jews, especially when the ghetto was created.

The Judenrat's most important role was to provide the German authorities with workers, according to their various demands. Different maneuverable and manip-ulatory attempts soon ensued and those close to the Jewish Council enjoyed its protection and were able to escape hard labor altogether. Departments and sections multiplied rapidly, creating a labyrinth of bureaucracy along the way.

A few days after the order was issued, the ghetto was closed. Any Jew who did not have a permit was not allowed to leave it. The ghetto was soon riddled with written warnings reading, "Do not climb! Entry prohibited!" But despite this explicit prohibition, Polish citizens came to the ghetto because it became a center for all commerce. A Jewish professional was cheaper to hire and better at his job, and groceries could be sold faster and at a higher price to the starving people of the ghetto.

A Jewish usher was stationed at every ghetto exit, tasked with checking permits and preventing people from leaving the area. The Ordnungsdienst's jurisdiction expanded and two headquarters were soon created and people paid a fortune to get to the *Ordnungsdienst* (the ghetto police). The *Ordenars* (officers) were not popular with the public. They served the German military police faithfully, diligently carrying out their orders.

This Ordnungsdienst was comprised mostly of what was previously referred to as "the golden youth." Those who did not want to serve the Germans—realizing the true nature of their assignments—refused, trading their personal interests for their dignity.

In many cases, the ushers would beat other Jews during a chase, as the Germans had managed to evoke their vilest instincts. This was one of the Germans objectives and unfortunately, it was achieved.

There were those among the Jews who collaborated

with them, the Jewish Council and its Ordnungsdienst serving at the most prominent examples of that cooperation. Apart from that, there were people who—for certain favors—would provide the Germans with information, such as where some Jews were hiding valuable possessions and the names of pre-war political activists. Despite their close cooperation with the Germans, however, these collaborators did not for the most part persevere: the German's methods did not allow them to live for very long and after they were no longer of any use, they suddenly "disappeared."

The people inside the ghetto attempted to lead a normal life, as much as it was possible. It was summer, and despite the hardships, every inch of land was cultivated. Everything was green, supporting the illusion of a normal life. The congestion, however, was very difficult: the Jews were crammed into a small area and the lack of housing was evident, with five to seven people often crammed into every room. There was also a critical food shortage: The most basic products cost a fortune and the needs of most people were not met. Agitation and squabbles grew more and more frequent, and anxiety and disquiet could be felt everywhere. The war's outlook was grim as it grew longer—and the longer it grew, the more brutal the Germans sanctions became.

But despite the difficult situation, culture was coming to life inside the ghetto. Concerts were held every Saturday and a youth club was formed. The poorest kids in the ghetto would spend most of their time in this club, where they could study and play, and even get a small meal.

Life in the ghetto was conducted amid a constant political debate. Even the media, which was banned by threat of death, was able to find its way into the near-occluded ghetto, including some radio transmitters; and in addition—despite a similar ban—a school system was created for the ghetto's youth.

In the early hours of every morning, long lines of Jews would leave the ghetto on forced labor assignments. At the beginning of 1940, the General Government, also known as the Generalgouvernement, issued an order regarding forced labor for all able-bodied Jews. The jobs were diverse and extremely difficult: river modulation, terrain development, and building bridges.

The Jewish Council allotted food portions for the workers from the ghetto's general food allowance. Large field kitchens were set up inside the ghetto, where the workers could receive a hot meal, usually made up of turnip and water. The lack of protein and fat was noticeable, people grew weaker due to malnutrition, and diseases ensued.

As the situation persisted, disease was rampant. Eventually, typhoid fever spread to the point where a special hospital had to be built to care for those infected by the contagious disease.

Mortality among the Jews was high and funerals were a common sight. The poor, who lived in the direst of conditions, suffered the most: hunger was compounded by refuse, and sanitation and clothing were scarce.

Winter was a particularly difficult time in the ghetto, as the hunger was accompanied by the bitter cold. The high price of coal left many apartments unheated, inflicting lung and kidney diseases on many, and the meager medical help available fell short of answering the people's needs.

The majority of the population made its living by selling personal effects. Business partnerships were formed for the purpose of buying such belongings and selling them in the Aryan part of town. Barter trades were also common, as the German farmers had little faith in money.

Religious life and traditional values all but disappeared in the ghetto. The Jewish youth conducted a frivolous life, believing that since there was no guarantee for tomorrow one must seize the day. Brothels were established as well, becoming a draw for many women because of the perpetual hunger. A small group of people in the ghetto, a clique of sorts, was very successful in their business and included, among others, intermediaries who were conducting shady deals. These people ran the risk of being caught by the Germans, knowing that those captured would be sent—at best— to a concentration camp.

Other financially privileged people in the ghetto were the members of the Jewish Council who lived a lavish lifestyle at the expense of their Jewish brothers.

That group included the Jewish police officers whose loyalty to the Germans prevented them from suffering any shortage.

The people in the ghetto were like caged animals, deprived of the ability to break out of its locked gates. The distress was most palpable during the spring, when everything was in bloom and the air in Częstochowa was rich with perfume. But to try and venture into nature was a death sentence. Those were daydreams, impractical thoughts. Reality offered much harsher, surreal images of wretched, miserable, individuals, who went out into the street to enjoy the early spring sun.

Here and there, one could see young men and women who would offer simple wares for sale, their calls of "saccharine, matches, cigarettes..." echoing along the street. A different group of young people could be seen on another street corner, relatively well dressed and talking among themselves. They were the cambists, the ones who regulated the black-market prices of goods. They placed themselves at risk, but they also made a profit.

Every now and then, a Jewish policeman would go by with his red hat, a yellow band and a rubber truncheon; elegantly dressed, in the spirit of the ghetto's war-like fashion: riding pants, a well-cut jacket and a well-tied necktie, sporting the "Ordenar" look. His head was usually held up high and his stride steadfast, the confidence he acquired clear, thanks to his role in the ghetto.

On the street leading to the train station, people

carrying packages and heading to the ghetto could always be seen. Those were the smugglers, carrying their goods and food from the Aryan into the ghetto for sale. The German military police would hold surprise raids on the road, scattering the vagabonds in all directions. But those who did not manage to get away were arrested and their merchandise was confiscated.

Unexpected pursuits in the streets would also take place: the Germans would demand a large number of people for labor, tasking the Ordnungsdienst with meeting the quota. Running and chasing would ensue, with ordenars yelling and arresting passersby, who were trying to hide as best as they could, in their attempt to meet the Germans' orders. Those who resisted were clubbed as they struggled against the police. After a few minutes, the street would become empty. The ushers were forced to remove people from their homes and the Jews' resistance made the mission difficult. Still, after a few hours, the required quota would be gathered. German cars arrived to pick up those who were caught for forced labor. As always, the policemen's acquaintances and those that bribed them were released. Protection and money—those were the most influential factors inside the ghetto.

The Germans wanted to maintain a constant sense of tension, turmoil, and uncertainty in the ghetto. To that aim, they would conduct periodic raids: in the early morning hours, certain streets would be surrounded by barricades, and German police, armed from head to toe, blocking them off from the other streets, barring anyone from entering or leaving the perimeter and enlisting the Jewish policemen to that effect. Fear befell the people inside the closed perimeter. It was not clear what the Germans were searching for this time or what should be removed from the house, as almost anything in it was in violation of some ban. Whether it was flour, sugar, butter or other dairy products, meat, oils or any other food—none of it could be kept because they were purchased on the black-market.

After a few hours, several limousines would appear, out of which stepped high-ranking policemen and Gestapo officials.

The search would commence. It turned out that someone informed the Germans that various types of leather were buried inside the closed perimeter. The information the Germans had was proven accurate and after a few hours of thorough searching, some leathers were found buried in several basements. A great deal of merchandise was discovered and trucks had to be brought in to carry them out.

Heated discussions were held about the conflict between Germany and the Soviets and the politicians in the ghetto often argued over it. It was said that German forces were amassing on the Soviet border. Many transporters were seen turning east and the trains were completely full with military officials and supplies, rushing to the Bug River. The German press was less preoccupied with the Soviet Union.

The previous praises in the press were gone. It was the calm before the storm, and the horizon was turning darker.

On June 22, 1941, the German armies attacked the Soviet Union. The war had changed and the two great nations were about to lock horns. It was a clash of two ideologies—communism and fascism—but which one would win? A few days earlier, trucks carrying war supplies passed through Częstochowa constantly, day and night. Now their purpose was clear. The expected clash between Germany and the Soviet Union created a great sense of anticipation among the Jews closed inside the ghettoes: They had always dreamed that the Soviet Union would declare war on the Germans. Everyone believed in the Soviets' great power and believed the Germans had grown weary after so many operations and would have to surrender. Their joy knew no limits and the Jewish "strategists" concluded that the Soviet battalions would be able to reach the ghetto within days. Everyone was sure of the Soviet Army's pending victory and no one wanted to believe that the outcome could be different.

But despite the war with the Soviets and the certainty in their victory on the front line, the Germans' attitude toward the Jews grew even worse. The German persecutions persisted and mass arrests took place almost every day. The prisoners would either be shot or sent to Auschwitz. Anyone who was suspected of being affiliated with a communist party before the war had to go into hiding. Even those that had relatives in the Soviet Union were not safe.

The Jews were disappointed. They did not know to what they should attribute the German's glorious triumphs. Could it be that the Soviet Union was really that weak? There were different theories but the truth was that no had the answer. German newspapers and loudspeakers announced victory and people spoke of the betrayal of the Ukrainians and the unorganized escape of the Soviet armies.

Amazed by their own success, the Germans did not change their attitude toward the Jews. All the hopes the Jews had for the German-Soviet war had faded. Depression and despair reigned anew and there were those who claimed that despite everything the Germans would fail, but when?

Meanwhile, the frequent raids caused the Jews to go out on the street only when there was no other choice. A hard winter came along. Ice covered everything, huge piles of snow collected on the streets and the roads. The living conditions were terrible and poverty, hunger and the cold were running rampant in the ghetto.

The Germans, after conquering vast territory in the Soviet Union, halted their attacks during the winter, as the soldiers of the Third Reich were not accustomed to the bitter eastern European cold. The Soviet armies seized the opportunity and switched to a winter attack. The German soldiers, who were sent to the front as auxiliary forces to the more distantly deployed German divisions and combat SS units, faced a difficult task. These legions passed through the ghetto causing people to flee the moment the first cars were seen. German assaults and the shooting of Jews multiplied.

The Germans led Soviet war prisoners through the streets of the ghetto. No one was allowed to approach them or hand them anything, and anyone who violated this order was sentenced to death. Rows of ragged characters in army uniforms plodded across the streets, surrounded by the German military police on all sides. The Jews, who were so looking forward to the Soviet soldiers' arrival, were sorely disappointed. The Soviet soldiers did come—but what a sad sight they made!

But the Soviets were not the only ones to suffer—the Germans suffered as well. The difficult winter in Russia that year was what troubled them the most: They were not properly prepared to deal with such climate conditions and frostbite took its toll on their limbs, ears and noses. Legions of soldiers passed through the ghetto and when such transports would arrive, the ghetto's streets would become empty within minutes. The Germans would vent their frustrations over their defeats on the front line by lashing out at the Jews.

***

Early 1942 brought with it the first signs that disaster was about to befall the Jews. During the first days of January, the SS and the Gestapo issued a merciless order: all the Jews, without exception, must hand over all the furs in their possession—long, short and fur collars too. Disobedience meant death.

Once the order was given, reinforced SS military police units appeared in the ghetto. People had to hand the furs to one of the residents of their house and they had to take them to a special warehouse. People knew that the German threat of death would be execute and therefore they had little choice but to obey. Yet there were always a few brave ones willing to take a risk and hide the furs, or smuggle them to the Aryan side. The Germans photographed the Jews as they surrendered their furs. Those photos were later published in their newspapers with captions reading, "Jews freely giving their furs to the German Army."

The battle between Germany and the Soviets continued on the front line. The troops at the front required supplies for the war, and the home front was tasked with feeding the war machine. The factories worked tirelessly to meet the military industry's demands. The Germans recruited the peoples of the nations they had conquered while they themselves usually filled administrative positions. The Jews were also enslaved in favor of the war effort and were forced to contribute their labor to the German victory. The irony!

All men ages 16-50 were forced to go to work. No exceptions were made. Special group permits were issued to that effect, because the work was conducted outside the ghetto. As time passed, the draft of labor forces increased, because the Germans were eyeing the eastern front. As the need for a work force intensified, retaliations in the ghetto increased as well. People in the ghetto lived in constant fear of raids, not only during the day, but also at night. Cultural activities were forsaken, only the club was still functioning.

The tension concentrated, with the political discussions between the Jews growing more heated, especially after Japan attacked the United States on December 7, 1941, and Germany's subsequent declaration of war on the United States. The war veered into a different direction and now loomed over Asia, Australia, and America as well. New hopes awoke in everyone, but those soon turned out to be false. The United States proved unable to help Europe and it suffered defeats at the hands of the Japanese. The proud German armies marched forward, mounting a new spring attack, conquering vast territories in Ukraine, Central Russia, and Crimea. In the ghetto, the situation became even worse.

Terrible news arrived from the eastern borders of Poland, saying that the Germans were killing all the Jews as soon as they set foot on its soil. Those who managed to escape and reach the ghetto recounted terrible stories of the slaughter against the Jews. The Germans and Ukrainians had gathered all the Jewish residents in a cemetery, where holes had been dug in advance and were ready for them, and shot them all dead. Mothers had to watch their babies being murdered, and children had to witness the death of their parents. The blood-thirsty Nazi beast was on the loose.

A dark shadow befell the residents of the ghetto, its residents distressed by the uncertainty about the fates of relatives or acquaintances. Spring was in bloom, as if the world was not in war, but the residents of the ghetto had neither the strength nor the will to welcome it. Rumors of mass murders and the establishment of death factories compounded the unbearable hardships.

And still, there were differences of opinion on the subject. The optimists claimed that it was impossible that in the 20th century, with the flourishing of civilization and the most advanced scientific and cultural achievements, a country would be able declare its intention to wipe out an entire people. The pessimists, however, believed the rumors were true. And the rumors were persistent. People discussed them frequently, and the names of the places where these *aktzias* (roundup of Jews from conquered territory for transport to death camps) had already claimed lives constantly were raised.

The Germans claimed that the Jewish residents merely relocated to the Ukrainian territories for labor, because the war had devastated those parts and there was a need for working hands. There were also those who believed the explanation: The German authorities had promised that it would not happen in the ghetto, as it excelled in productive work that served the needs of the war. That promise was followed by a rumor, spread by the Jewish Council, that whoever works would be protected from the transfers. Many people made a special effort to get as much work as possible while others were willing to pay large sums of money for a place to hide.

The *arbeitsamt* (employment bureau) issued *arbeitskarten* (special work permits). Whoever was employed in a certain factory would receive a stamp on his work permit, reaffirming his status. But it was not enough and the arbeitskarte also had to be signed by the arbeitsamt. The second signature was harder to get, because it was only given to those who worked in the factories that supplied the needs of the war. But money was of use again for those that had it. For now.

Toward the end of July 1942, on a marvelously sunny Saturday, the military police and the Polish police surrounded the ghetto. Great panic spread when people saw what was going on in the morning, because they thought it was an aktzia. But it turned out that it was just a trial-run. The Germans issued an order that all men ages 16-55 were to report to the market square at a designated hour. Afterward, the military police searched the apartments. The streets emptied, not one living soul was seen. From time to time, the shadow of an armed military policeman with a steel helmet would pass by.

A sea of people could be seen in the two market squares, their disquiet, and anxiety obvious. At last, the chief arbeitsamt inspector arrived with several top military police officers. The workers gathered and in turn, went to work without knowing what the Germans will do to those who remained in the market square and those who remained in their homes. The anxiety grew stronger and the day grew unbearably long.

Those who did not leave for work were led to an abandoned factory. No one knew what would happen to them and while different rumors circulated in the ghetto, nothing was clear. After a few days, the prisoners joined different work posts and were released to their homes. Only later it became clear that it was a preview of a real aktzia that was about to take place. The Germans benefited from this test-run: They learned to gauge people's reaction to the aktzia and even learned the number of workers in the ghetto. It was their first "technical trial."

The large ghetto in Warsaw was destroyed by then. There was no more doubt about its residents' fate. Messengers sent by the Warsaw underground came to the Jewish Council of Częstochowa and presented them with fact about the new reality, offering to organize some protection for the Jews. The council not only refused, it never even informed the residents of the offer.

Days filled with anticipation and foreboding passed. By then, it was common knowledge that special battalions comprised of Ukrainian mercenaries participated in these aktzias. These Ukrainian mercenaries were infamously more sadistic than the Germans. The main issue discussed in the ghetto was what was going on in the Warsaw ghetto and whether it could happen in Częstochowa. Politics took second place now, even if in the meantime Germany conquered vast territories in the Soviet Union. They had reached the Caucasus on one side and Moscow on the other and for the first time in history, the Germans had reached the Volga River.

Toward the end of September, the bitter truth was revealed: the Ukrainians had arrived. There was no doubt now that this ghetto was doomed. Everyone wondered the same thing: what will tomorrow bring?

Aktzia

On Yom Kippur 1942, despite the day's sanctity, everyone was rushing to work. The arrival of the Ukrainians confirmed our greatest fears. The ghetto was steaming and stirring, uncertainty and anxiety taking even the greatest optimists over.

The devout, who did not go to work due to the holiness of the day, as well as the elderly, held fervent prayer services in different apartments that served as temporary houses of worship throughout the ghetto. An ominous feeling of danger was in the air and the sound of lamenting cries could be heard from the apartments. The women were praying as well. The Germans, who knew it was a holy day, conducted a raid focused on these makeshift houses of worship. People with talits on their shoulders attempted to escape through the doors and windows. The sight was appalling: old men trying to run as the Germans, mocking and amused, chased them.

After some of the worshipers were taken for labor, rumors started to come from the Jews who went to work outside the ghetto. They had heard from the Poles about the Jewish massacre in Warsaw and other cities, about the unusual cruelty of the Ukrainians. There were even rumors that said that an aktzia was about to take place in Częstochowa. The atmosphere was morose. Everyone wanted to get home as fast as possible, to be with his or her relatives. The hours grew long and the work was not progressing as usual. When the Germans sensed it and sought an explanation, they were told that there was fear of an aktzia; they laughed, dismissing the as untrue.

The slave-workers finally returned to their homes and told their families what they had heard from the Poles. Anxiety throughout the ghetto increased even more.

Another raid took place in the afternoon. The Germans had a particular goal, to distract the attention of the Jewish population from what they were planning. Military Police Captain Paul Degenhart, who was in charge of the ghetto, gave the Jewish Council his word of honor that he had no knowledge of any such plan. The news of Degenhart's phone call spread through the ghetto immediately, but it was of little solace.

The following day, he was the one who led the murderous aktzia in the ghetto and in three other cities.

People gathered in front of their homes, trying to calm each other down, although they themselves did not believe in their own arguments. Anxiety increased as the evening approached and the arrival of senior SS officials from Radom County, whose job was to oversee the aktzia the next day, was widely discussed. There was no doubt that what people had feared the most was now inevitable. The Polish police officers, who stood armed at the exits from the ghetto, confirmed people's fears.

Anyone who could turn to someone on the Aryan side tried to escape the ghetto. Parents sent their children to Polish acquaintances, often for money, pleading with them to shelter the children in their homes while the aktzia in the ghetto continued. This night of anticipation, a night of despair, will forever be etched in the memory of anyone who survived it. The only sure thing was that the children, those fragile, innocent creatures, would be the ones to die first. Many of them were not even aware of the fact that they were Jews, their parents were already murdered, and there was no one to come and claim them. People prepared bunkers to hide in, taking their most valuable possessions there in secret, so their hiding place was not revealed. Disorder reigned in every apartment, backpacks and bundles were packed with haste; from time to time, someone glanced nervously at the person next to him. Will we see each other tomorrow? No one spoke; everyone understood that danger surrounded them all equally, without exception.

It was the morning of September 22, 1942. It was still dark when Degenhart ordered the Jewish ushers, the Ordnungsdienst, to assemble. It was an ominous sign.

This was really happening!

The ushers had already gathered inside the headquarters. A thick ring of SS, Ukrainians, military police, and Polish police personnel surrounded the ghetto. Not only were all the street exits blocked, but inside the ghetto neighborhoods were cut off from one another. The Jewish ushers went from street to street, from house to house, announcing the German orders: everyone, without exceptions—young and old, women and children—are to report to a set place. They are allowed to carry no more than 10 kilograms of luggage. Those that had a work permit signed by the employment bureau and the factory where they worked, were called in to report to the former metallurgical factory. After the Germans checked their papers, they were let inside the factory. They were also told to take a change of clothes and food for two days.

People obeyed. From time to time, loud cries and women's wailing were heard. The ushers announced—whoever fails to leave his house by nine o'clock, will be shot on sight.

This was the onset of hell. The "lucky ones," those who had a work permit with two signatures, did not want to say goodbye to their families; and their wives, mothers and fathers, brothers and sisters were begging them at least to save themselves, while there was still a chance. Hectic arguments mingled with crying were taking place, and heartbreaking goodbyes could be seen everywhere.

The streets were full of people rushing in different directions, but the Ukrainians at the gates brought them back to the round-up point.

A crowd amassed in front of the metallurgical factory to get inside, but only those who had a signed permit—meeting the Germans' demands—were allowed to enter. At first, the young and the old were allowed inside, but when the Germans noticed that more people than they anticipated had entered, they started to conduct a more diligent selection; allowing only the young and those who appeared healthy to enter the premises. They simply tore the rest of the work permits and sent their owners to the general round-up point for transfer. Many young people whose permits were in order decided to go with their relatives and instead of going to the metallurgy hall, they headed to the round-up point.

Nevertheless, in some tragic cases, although rare, mothers abandoned their children to save their own lives. Future aktzias would see more such cases.

When the quota of people sought by the Germans for the first aktzia was achieved, they made the others run to the gathering point. A cruel game began: the Jews, burdened with their bundles, their children in their arms, were made to run through the streets, which were lined with SS officers, military policemen and Ukrainians and Polish soldiers—all armed with an automatic weapon and clubs.

How different their persecutors seemed, with a glint of sadistic amusement in their eyes and a grin on their faces, as they mercilessly hit the people running before them with the butts of their rifles and their clubs.

Those left at the metallurgical factory gate exchanged

pained glances, but they were not even allowed to cry in despair—the Germans would have none of that. The workers were brutally scattered, clubs and rifles jabbing at their heads when suddenly, a gunshot was heard. One of the young men failed to obey the order and fell to the ground, his body riddled with bullet holes. Not everyone managed to arrive at the gathering point when the shooting began. People were still on the streets.

The Ukrainians, the SS officers and the military policemen started "touring" the ghetto. They went from house to house, going through all the apartments, basements, and attics in search for Jews. They came across an old man, who was too sick and exhausted to get to the collection point. A short volley from an automatic weapon and it was "game over."

The body of a woman lay in the street, the bodies of her two children beside her. For reasons unknown she did not manage to leave by nine o'clock, and when she came out to the street, she was met by gunshots. She was lying dead in the street, still clutching her children in her disfigured arms. An appalling sight could be seen in one of the yards: a young man and a young woman attempted to hide, but were discovered. They were tortured and beheaded, their headless bodies just left there. A small group was suddenly seen coming back from the round-up point. Were they allowed to come back? A glimmer of hope flickered for a moment, but no—it was only due to the lack of room in the car. The Germans crammed 120 people into each car and they could not carry anymore. More than 5,000 people were crammed into some 50-60 cars.

When the shooting began, the SS and police officers started counting those gathered at the metallurgical factory. The "chosen" ones stood there with their heads bowed down. They had no homes, no families and they were at the mercy—or lack thereof—of their enemies. At best, they could hope for a new existence, full of humiliation, pain, and loneliness.

The first shipment of those who were deported was on its way and the sounds of gunfire inside the ghetto were gradually subsiding. Many people were taken out of their hiding places and murdered, but many did not bother hiding at all. They preferred death to enduring the torture of the death shipment. Hundreds of bodies littered the streets and yards.

The residents of the ghetto, who were not included in the first aktzia, were completely cut off from those that were in the factory, and from the rest of the world. They had to fend for themselves and find food with no supply from the outside and no stipend of any kind. Meanwhile, in the old metallurgical factory, the Jewish Council and its proxies were trying to introduce some kind of order at the plant and organize a kitchen. The Jewish ushers, who were still allowed to move across the ghetto, brought those who remained there the different news.

On the first day, people in metallurgy were tasked with removing the bodies from the streets. One of the

Jewish ushers received an order to gather a few dozen men and went to work with them. In the afternoon, a manager from *Hasag*, a new arms factory, and his escorts arrived in the ghetto in their cars. A selection process began: The young and the healthy were made to march in front of the officials, who decided if they were fit for work or not. Some, either those who were too young or for other reasons, were passed over. Those who were chosen were immediately surrounded by the factory guards, the *werkschutz*, and taken to Hasag shortly thereafter.

In the evening, when the workers who were sent to bury the dead brought the bodies back, one of the Jews was forced to search them, in the presence of a military policeman, and hand him the dead's belongings and any valuables or money that were found on them. If a ring could not be removed from a finger, the police officer would cut the finger off to remove it. Some "undertakers," however, brought back only few valuables. Vultures can be found in every disaster.

The next day, after a night of disquiet and gunfire, people were moved through the different working stations, mainly military ones, as the army was the only ones eligible to use Jews for labor. The Germans no longer viewed the Jews as humans. They became labor material with no human value. No one had the right to choose, no one had the right to express a different opinion or to object, because it usually led to torture, which was followed by a death sentence—a "shipment to Palestine," as the Germans liked to joke.

There was an eerie silence on the ghetto's empty streets broken only by the occasional Ukrainian or military policeman passing through. People were warned not to look through the windows—the guards liked shooting at windows. The remaining residents of the ghetto were enduring their tragedy in silence.

After the three days of the first aktzia, it was time for the rest of the ghetto. Now they were all made to go to the marketplace and pass by Degenhart, who oversaw the aktzia with a whip in his hand and a smile on his face. A flick of the whip to the right meant "stay" and a flick to the left meant "ship." Naturally, the majority of the Jews were directed to the left. Those who remained were but a few and were seemingly both young and healthy. Dante-like scenes took place as mothers cajoled their children into going to save their lives. The Germans would not allow it, nor did they allow young people who were meant for the shipments to go with their relatives. Those who remained were sent to join those inside the old metallurgical factory. They had managed to scare up some food there, but it required standing in line for hours.

In the newly emptied part of the ghetto, the Germans ransacked the banished Jews' property: food, furniture that was in good shape, carpets, linen, and chandeliers. The hunt for people in hiding continued relentlessly, hunger and thirst forcing them out of hiding in search of food and water. Elderly people, from the few streets that were still inhabited came to metallurgy. The undertakers had constant employment. The "transfer" kept everyone busy, military policemen, Polish police officers, and Jewish ushers—for good money, of course, foreign currency or gold.

There was great hunger inside the ghetto. An aktzia was a lengthy process, taking several days at a time, and there were no food supplies. Those who were able to stock some food managed somehow, but the majority starved. The disaster united people and committees were formed, collecting food from all the residents and portioning it out to everyone. Soon, however, those stocks were gone as well.

Finally, the third and fourth aktzias had come. Each one was worse than the ones before it, until only a handful of people remained. It was a horrific sight! People would approach the Germans, who determined life or death, in fear. Young people, in their prime, were walking toward their death. They could have contributed so much, not only to the Jewish people, but to the entire world!

Until then, these aktzias did not include the families of policemen from the ghetto, even though Degenhart sent some of them to work at Hasag and others were demoted and deported.

The Jews that stayed inside the ghetto were sent to the labor stations. The worst station was in Hasag. The conditions there were appalling; not only in terms of food and hard labor, but also in terms of how the factory guards, the *werkschutz*, and the German work managers treated the workers. Anguish amplified the great hunger and fatigue and it was almost too difficult to bear. The groups that were stationed in the military posts were in relatively better living conditions and were treated better. But that could not be said about the Jews who were stationed under the supervision of the SS or the military police. They saw in every Jew the reason for the calamities of the German people. Verbal and physical abuse was common, as was the crack of a whip, which often hit the people who "were to blame for this war."

In metallurgy, the recruitment for Hasag workers continued, for no one wanted to go there. The Jewish ushers went out of their way to meet the German demand, deluding themselves into believing that they could protect their families and themselves from the shipments that way. By this time, the murderous aktzia had been going on for two weeks, imposing an atmosphere of terror and death on the ghetto. The search for those who were in hiding continued relentlessly. During one of these aktzias, Degenhart made the selection for metallurgy. Everyone was taken outside and a thorough search was conducted inside the building. Afterward, the oldest people were ordered to join the shipment.

The Germans used special measures to kill those who were hospitalized in the ghetto's general hospital and contagious diseases clinic. They used phenol—a powerful anesthetic drug—which the Jewish doctors had to forcibly administer to the patients. After a while, the undertaker squadron was called in to collect the bodies and haul them to mass graves. There were those who were not dead and begged their executioners to shoot them—to no avail.

The Jewish ushers' turn came during the last aktzias. More than half of them were deported with their families and only a handful of them got to leave their wives and children in the ghetto.

After three and a half weeks, the ghetto was liquidated. Still, many people remained there—more than the SS had intended. The Germans used different tricks to lure those that were in hiding out in the open, including the promise of redemption: "If you leave on your own, you will live!" they cajoled. Jewish ushers ran from house to house shouting: "Leave, brothers! You are free, the aktzia has ended!" Those who were in hiding were tortured by the lack of air, food, and water, as well as paralyzing fear, so many of them came out. They were immediately arrested and led to a special location, where an aktzia was underway.

Rumors sparked that the Jews were being sent to their death. People spoke about Treblinka, gas chambers and the execution of thousands of Jews. The news was so monstrous and surreal that people refused to believe it and heated debates were conducted as to their credibility. The majority of people did not believe the rumors. The concern for the fate of loved ones, however, was shared by all, and this gradually grew into total despair.

The Ukrainians played a key role in the series of aktzias. Anywhere where torture and anguish needed to be applied, a Ukrainian would deliver it with pleasure. They would hang around, drunk for most of the time, as the Germans never denied them any Vodka. Every Ukrainian had a few watches and rings that were either robbed from Jews or removed from those who were murdered. They competed with the SS officers, the military policemen, and the Polish policemen for the loot.

During the weeks of the aktzias, 40,000 Jews were deported from the Częstochowa ghetto, mostly to the Treblinka death camp. Toward the end of the aktzia, the few who managed to escape Treblinka came back and shared what they knew about what was going on. No one wanted to believe them, but as the weeks went by and none of those who were sent away showed any sign of life, the horrible truth became clear.

When these aktzias took place in the Jewish quarter, people from the other side of Częstochowa would gather on the other side of the barricade to watch the tragedy of the city's Jews unfold. Sympathy was not to be expected, on the contrary, there was a satisfied smile on many faces over Poland's "cleansing" of the Jews. Toward the end of October, the remaining 5,000 Jews who were left in the city were put into what was called the "small ghetto," where they tried to rebuild their lives. Only the young ones and the adult members of the Jewish Council remained, alongside a few doctors and some ghetto ushers.

Another era had begun inside the ghetto.

The Jewish Resistance in Częstochowa

1942. There were two youth movements in Częstochowa and both groups—which had already formed into kibbutzim, belonged to *Żydowska Organizacja Bojowa* (ŻOB)—the Jewish Combat Organization.

Two events connected to their activity remain particularly set in my memory. On January 4, 1943, people left the ghetto for work. The Germans conducted a raid in search of those who remained in the ghetto. They gathered them near the entrance to the ghetto and were about to send them to Radomsk, and from there to Treblinka. Two ŻOB members, Mendel Fiszlewicz and Izak Fajner, were among them and both of them were armed. Fiszlewicz attacked a police captain by the name of Rohn, who was conducting the aktzia and Fajner pointed his gun at another officer. Both fighters were shot on the spot. People said that the ŻOB members' guns, which were bought on the Aryan side, did not function properly.

The Ostbahn Aktzia

The ŻOB base in Częstochowa was on 71 Nadrzeczna Street. One day, they decided to conduct an act of sabotage against the Nazis and derail a German train traveling on the Ostbahn—the eastern railway. To that end, they had to get a special key to access the tracks. ŻOB member Maria Szlezinger helped fabricate such a key during one of her shifts in a German factory. She was in the middle of her mission when all of a sudden the German work manager entered, looked at what she had on her desk, said nothing, and left. She was sure she was doomed, but later, the German only said, "I didn't see anything and I don't want to know anything."

The person who came up with the idea to sabotage the train was Zvi Lustiger. The fighters organized in a foursome: Zvi Lustiger, David Landau, Frenkenberg and Aviv Rosner. When the usual group of 48 men was taken to work on the Ostbahn train, the four joined them. It was toward the end of March or the beginning of April 1943. Frenkenberg left them along the way. The four had to find an opportunity to dismantle the tracks. They tried to get as close as they could to the tracks but a Ukrainian werkschutz, one of the railway guards, noticed a suspicious movement among the Jewish workers, searched one of them and found the key. He immediately reported the incident, and the police and the Gestapo appeared on the scene. They counted the workers and instead of 48, they found 52. The commander of the ŻOB sabotage cell assumed the blame for the operation. David Landau attempted to escape and was shot. A gun was found on Zvi Lustiger and the Germans interrogated and tortured him for a long time to find out whether he arrived with the group of workers. He could not speak but shook his head in denial. The Germans shot the other two Nadrzeczna ŻOB members. As for the other 48 Ostbahn workers— the Gestapo wanted to kill all of them, but the railway guards agreed to kill every other one. After some discussion, they reached an agreement: they chose every other worker in the line and shot him. That way, more than 20 people were killed. My schoolmate Lewek Jakubowicz was among those who survived that day. He made it to live in Israel and I confirmed my memories with him.

My brother Heniek and I were working in a factory at Landau at the time, not far from the ghetto. We heard these gunshots. When we returned from work, the bodies were already gone, but the snow was red with blood.

From the Memories of Heniek Wodzislawski (1923-2004)

My brother, Yehiel—Heniek Wodzislawski—kept notes with exact descriptions of certain events in our lives during the Nazi occupation. After my brother died, I kept his notes. I decided to add them to this book.

Part One and Part Two: from the diary written by my brother, Yehiel-Heniek Wodzislawski, R.I.P.

Part One

On Saturday, June 26, 1943, at 11 a.m. the Jewish police notified the Jewish population that remained in the ghetto that the men were required to gather in the small marketplace. People could feel that the ghetto was about to be liquidated. There were those who were deluding themselves into thinking that the Germans would only search the houses, a thorough and in-depth search. We may be left at the station and we will return later. For it was not possible that we would be bound for the barracks in Hasag—they had yet to build them—so where will they put us all? Where would we sleep?

The cover of my brother's notebook.

People were coming out, but the Jewish police did not allow them to take any parcels. There were relatively few people, as those who were employed in Hasag, about 2,000 people, were detained there. Many of the residents decided not to go out, because of their parents and children, hiding in bunkers instead. People from the resistance group were almost invisible. Some of those who were taken by the Germans the day before managed to exit through the tunnel on Saturday night. The rest, whom everybody knew, did not want to appear in public—they were afraid someone would turn them in to the Germans. Therefore, only a few of those who were in hiding, those who did not have many acquaintances among the residents, came out.

We were standing in the small marketplace. We were organized in groups of five, creating three sides of a rectangle. The road from the ghetto to Warszawska Street was to our side. This was the stage on which another tragedy in the lives of the Częstochowa's Jews was about to unfold.

I was looking toward the ghetto. Different types of forces were deployed in the city: there was the military police, the Gestapo, pilots, Wehrmacht, Ukrainians, the Polish police and who knows what else. And almost everyone was armed with automatic weapons.

These brutes densely surrounded the ghetto. A fully armed military police unit stood in the corner of the small marketplace. They came in cars, which were still standing on the road, and in the middle of the square *stood the principle director — Degenhart — whom we all knew, with his entourage, each of them more monstrous and murderous than the next. Next to them stood the chief of Gestapo, a captain of the Wehrmacht and a captain in the air force — each with their own entourage.*

The women, meanwhile, were crammed into a little plaza near the ghetto's exit, where the Jewish police guarded them. Scared, their eyes begged the question: what will become of us?

Degenhart inspected the lines, singling out the elderly and the children. This continued for several few minutes. The first shipment of the innocent victims of the Nazi regime was loaded into one of the military police cars and taken away. Then Degenhart called Bernard Kurland, the manager of the Jewish Employment Bureau and ordered him to read the list of those who were called to step forward. He read more than 10 names but no one stepped forward. Degenhart approached Kurland and quietly told him something. Kurland then hid the list and announced, "On Degenhart's command, all those that live on 86 and 88 Nadrzeczna Street, step forward."

The rows started moving and people stepped out and stood in groups of five on the side. There were about twenty of them, but that was not enough for Degenhart. He reproached Kurland, who entered the ghetto and called the Jewish policeman in charge of block 86-88 on Nadrzeczna Street, a man called Goldberg. He stood before Degenhart, who explained something to him. Afterward, Goldberg reviewed the lines with a Gestapo official, pointing out those who lived on his block.

The Gestapo official, pointing his gun at people's faces, said in a sweet and cynical tone, "Come out on your own, because whoever doesn't come out now, and will be pointed out to us later, will suffer more." More and more people stepped out. The Jewish cop and the Gestapo official walked through the lines until a group of 80 individuals was standing on the side. Every one of the people standing in the small marketplace was wondering: What will happen next? What will they do with us? A truck arrived and the policemen ordered the group to get inside. Everyone knew what that meant: the Nazi vampire was thirsty for blood! Horror and sorrow enveloped the men standing there as those who were selected refused to board the truck.

All of a sudden, a larger group of military officers surrounded them and cocked their weapons. They then began kicking the Jews and beating them with their rifles.

Finally, screaming, cursing, and sobbing, people were loaded onto the truck. They knew where they were going and they had different reactions to it: Some bit their lips, clutched their fists nervously with a dark look on their faces. "Friends, we are going to our deaths, avenge us!" they shouted at us.

Others on the truck were moving nervously, cursing the Germans and the Nazi regime, waving their fists at the military policemen, yelling, "It won't help you, anyway, executioners, murderers, criminals." Some pleaded with the Germans, sobbing that they had wives and that they were young and want to live. But they soon fell silent, seeing that it made no impression the Germans. Some were mumbling confession-like prayers before death.

The women, who were standing near the ghetto's exit were lamenting aloud. The men left standing in the small marketplace were silent, indifferent-looking, only their eyes were fervent. Their fists were clutched as their hearts were torn with unbearable pain. Some had tears in their eyes and they had lowered their heads. We were helpless.

The truck's engine was humming. Military officers boarded the truck as escorts, but seeing the faces and fists of the condemned men, they did not want to take any risks and got off, boarding another car while pointing their guns and rifles at the truck. As the cars started to move a terrible cry was heard from the truck — they were going away for good — and with this cry, the innocent victims' last sound, only two sentences could be discerned, overcoming all others: "Shema Israel!" and "Friends, avenge us!" The cars turned to Warszawska Street and after a moment, gunshots were heard. They were aimed at people who were jumping off the truck, which was speeding away. It seemed that some managed to escape. Almost no one reached the cemetery. The road was riddled with bodies.

We were standing, waiting for what was to happen next. The commander of the factory guard, Markov Pfeiffer, arrived with his deputy, Milof and the guards.

After a moment, Lidet, the manager of the Hasag-Platzer factory, and Pfeiffer were followed by Fabricius and his gang of factory guards.

We then learned what they were going to do with us: we were going to Hasag, to the German factories. Milof chose about 300 men that were about to go to the factories in Rakow. There were many more volunteers for Rakow, because Milof was known as a "good German." The rest of the people had to go to Peltzery.

The Germans were now conducting raids, ordering everyone to hand in their money, gold and any other valuables, under threat of death. Some handed it over, some hid it and others, who were too afraid to hide their possessions but were also unwilling to give them up, tore everything to pieces or threw them under their feet and stomped on everything that could be destroyed.

People were still undergoing selection during the raids. The Germans chose a few elderly people and about 100 boys ages 10-15, and set them aside. The boys' mothers, who were standing at the ghetto's exit, were shouting and crying out loud, unable to control their grief.

The raid continued. Military policemen were passing through the crowd with Degenhart and choosing Jews who were once useful to them, those who once served at the security police's headquarters on 14 Avenue Garibaldi Street. The first group that was chosen for Rakow was underway escorted by the factory guards.

The second group, which was meant for Peltzery,

was now standing in line. We were about 1,500 people. There were about 300 people left in the small market-place, chosen by the military policemen and they had to go to Garibaldi Street. Degenhart ordered the older men and the boys to get on the truck, but the manager, Lidet, protected the youngsters and took the boys to the Pelt-zery factory.

The line moved in groups of five. The Jews were walking toward a new period in their lives, maybe their last. They were walking grimly and silently, like in a funeral procession, while around them the shouts of the escorting factory guards could be heard and people on the street were looking at them curiously.

Among the Jewish men, only the police and some of the management remained in the ghetto, to help the Germans "sort" through the women. But the women were not facing the unknown—they knew exactly what the process meant and where the others were going, and often, a sister who did not want to say goodbye, or a daughter who did not want to leave her mother, went together toward a shared death or additional hardships. The women were sent to the same workstations the men had occupied before.

The Jewish police and the residents of the bunkers remained in the ghetto. The former had to find and hunt down the latter. A brother had to hand his own brother over to the executioners.

When we arrived at Peltzery, other Jews were already waiting for us—they were those who were left from the day before and were detained in the factory, unable to return to the ghetto. They asked us about the latest events in the ghetto. We told them that the ghetto had already been liquidated and that we were not going back there. Cries and heavy sighs were heard, followed by questions and answers. The mood was dark, and a state of despair and uncertainty came over people. Everyone lost someone, and trepidation could be seen on everyone's faces.

It was noon. We received coupons for lunch and bread. Long lines were standing in front of the kitchen, waiting for the diluted, meager, and tasteless soup. Too little bread was handed out—200 grams per person. Hunger was felt from the very first day and it grew worse and intolerable with time. They brought lunch from the ghetto, cooked from the supplies that were left there, but that did not solve the problem. Bread prices were very high, about 100 Zloty per 2 kilograms. We were sleeping in empty halls and warehouses, without mattresses, only on holzwolle (wood shavings).

On the second day of our arrival at the factory, the newcomers were sent to work. Each section had to wear a different-color armband and we were divided into groups of 30 men, with a Kapo in charge of putting all of the group's affairs in order. The manager of Hasag, Lidet, addressed those who were already assigned to a Kapo, and he claimed that we were responsible for being arrested and placed in the camp, due to our "revolutionary activities."

He warned us against the desire to organize anything similar in the factory and promised us that if we worked well, he would try to provide us with the best possible conditions. Afterward, he addressed the baubetrieb *(construction workers) and ordered them to build barracks where we would be better off as fast as possible. That was the beginning of life in Hasag. A routine was slowly taking shape: we were ordered to wake up at 5 a.m., bathe and then organize the sheds and stand for the morning census. We would then report to the supervisors for work, which started at 7 a.m. Breakfast was from 9-9:15 a.m. and consisted of 200 grams of dark bread and coffee. Lunch lasted half an hour, from 12:30 to 1 p.m. and consisted of half a liter of diluted soup. Work usually continued until 5:45 p.m., when watery soup was handed out again. We were ordered to go to sleep at 9 p.m.*

Work at the production lines was conducted in two shifts. The work was hard and entailed great responsibility; it was supervised by a German foreman and for every offense—and more often than not with no reason at all—people were beaten or led to the guard house, where the guards, werkschutz, *would mercilessly abuse them.*

The Kapos handed us the bread after receiving it from the managers. The Innendienst *(Jewish Interior Service), which handed out all the stipends, would hand it out with coupons for lunch in every section. The Interior Service was supervised by the* Einzatz *(Jewish*

Employment Bureau), headed by A. Kurland. Alongside the Einzatz, there was also the Jewish Order Service, made up of five people and some of their peers from the ghetto. Each section had one and they had to oversee all of the workers' affairs.

Life for the Jews in Hasag was full of labor, hunger, fear, and thoughts of a very unhappy future. The end of the war was nowhere in sight and first we had to survive winter in Hasag. The hunger grew every day—they were not bringing us lunches from the ghetto anymore—and bread was becoming more and more expensive because of the searches the Poles underwent when they came into the factory.

People's clothes were worn out, and there were no replacements. The sanitary conditions were steadily worsening.

The question on everyone's mind was Will we survive? News from the outside was only adding to the general depression. The Germans discovered many bunkers inside the ghetto and killed all the people that were hiding in them. Afterward, a "pardon" was granted to those who came out on their own, but those who believed it and came out were murdered. They were now burning down the ghetto. The explosions from the buildings blown up were heard all over.

In the meantime, some utensils and beddings were brought and divided among the people, but it was insufficient, and no one was happy about it because the hunger was stronger than anything else. People were exhausted from hard labor and insufficient food, and times when people fainted from hunger during work were becoming more and more common. In such a situation, Lidet would issue a permit to sell bread to the Jews, and dark bread would be made available in the employment bureau for 40 Zloty per 2 kilos. The hunger nightmare was over for whoever had money and the general mood improved.

This situation continued for several weeks.

In the meantime, the ghetto was completely liquidated and the Jewish police moved to Garibaldi Street. The question was what will become of them? No one had to wait long for an answer. Those that served the Germans faced a wretched end: one day, there was a census of men and women for shipment to the Rakow factory. An observant spectator could see it was a sign, but the majority did not suspect anything.

In the evening, the Hasag Jewish police alongside the ghetto's police, as well as the entire staff from the employment bureau were called to the guarding post. They went there but they did not return. A general assembly was called for 10 p.m. and panic suddenly possessed everyone—what did it mean? What are they planning to do with us? The lines stretched on the main road to the factory and guards were standing on both sides. A powerful streetlamp was hanging on one of the streets, lighting the location where people would be sorted for life or death.

After a few tense moments, the manager, Lidet, arrived with Lasinski, the military officer, and the commander of the factory guard, and with them the obermeister (head manager) of the different departments. They all stood under the streetlamp. The lines marched before them, section after section, absorbing the horrible word "selection." The elderly, the crippled and anyone else the Germans did not like were set aside.

Group after group, in fives, they marched before the obermeister in that lit spot. They looked at the people's faces, dragging someone else aside each time. The rows seemed silent and obedient. Was there a selection in the factory too? Was death lurking for us here as well?

The selection process lasted for two hours. Those who were chosen were locked down in the hall and later led to a basement in Kolonia, an area near the factory, where the workers lived. The rest were told to go back to sleep, but no one slept that night. There were only sighs, sobs, crying and complaints, curses and threats. One person was crying for his father, another's sister was taken, that one lost his wife, and the other could not find his friend anymore. There were those that did not want to say goodbye to their relatives so a husband followed his wife, a daughter followed her mother, and a sister followed her sister. They preferred to die together.

The next day, everybody went to work and we saw that the Jewish police and the employment bureau did not return and that the Germans took all of the management workers and some of the medical staff. Despair took over the factory. More news revealed that the Germans brought all of the ghetto police to Kolonia and put them in the basement. *They brought some cars from Garibaldi Street, too, and those cars were about to take people to the cemetery. But the people, who aware of their fate, were courageously resisting. The Germans, fearing that the Jews would be able to fend them off and run away, attempted to stun them on the spot and tie them to the cars headed to the cemetery. But their plan was still not executed easily as the men resisted as best as they could. The Germans recruited all of the factory guards to help them: they stunned each of the Jews with a hammer blow to the back of the head, tied their hands behind their backs with a metal wire and threw them inside the cars.*

The cars left one after the other to the cemetery, and came back empty to take new victims. And in the factory, work was performed "as usual," but the Jews were restless. Anxiety and disquiet could be felt in the air. People were whispering to one another and passing news by word of mouth.

The anxiety was growing. It lasted two days and then nerves were replaced with hesitation. People stopped trusting tomorrow and escape attempts grew more frequent. Meanwhile, a new employment bureau was forming with Zilberman as its manager. A new internal administrative service was formed, as was a laundry room and a steam room in the bathhouse. Life carried on. The first barracks were built and people moved there in groups. A fence made of two rows of barbed wire was put up around the barracks. One of the sheds was organized as a hospital and a first-aid station and another shed, which was somewhat removed from the rest, was designated as an infectious diseases clinic. Outside that territory, Jews were only living in one hall that was dubbed the "Circus."

And so, life in Hasag continued with the occasional beatings, visits to the guardroom and bodily searches. No one was selling bread anymore, but it could be bought from the Poles that came to the factory.

At the same time, people were also coming in from Garibaldi Street. They had many possessions, which they exchanged for money, and that way put some money in Jewish hands. Self-help committees were formed in the different departments without the Germans' knowledge. The sad and monotonous life in Hasag continued and their bleakness was relieved only by news from the outside.

We learned about Italy's surrender. There was an optimistic mood in the factory. Maybe the Germans, like the Italians, would crack from within and we would be saved? We were expecting such a moment but it never came. A shipment of several dozen men from Rakow, however, did, with news about our brothers. After several weeks, panic stirred up the factory again: the Germans said they needed 39 people for a shipment to Piotrków, but who knew where they would send them? The next day, after those 39 people left, the rest of the Jews from Garibaldi Street arrived. They were living in Hasag now, but about 30 of them were going out every *day under the werkschutz's guard to work at the security police's headquarters.*

The people from Garibaldi Street were those among us who were well off, since they had clothes and money in abundance and at that time, they did not have nutritional problems. It was extremely difficult for the rest of the people.

Used clothes and wooden clogs that the Germans allotted arrived and again, there was not enough to go around. Everyone tried to get by somehow, tailors sewed after work hours for the Poles, milliners were making hats, cobblers were making and selling shoes, and people were making and selling small metal objects. Tinsmiths, locksmiths, watchmakers, goldsmiths, carpenters, hairdressers—everyone was trying to earn something in their profession, getting by as best they could. And yet, the hunger was persistent. Cases of tuberculosis were becoming more frequent. Whoever was infected was doomed: after several weeks' worth of stay in the contagious diseases clinic, without proper conditions, the majority died. The dead were taken to the Jewish cemetery and buried there.

A general vaccination was held in order to prevent contagious diseases from spreading. A special field kitchen was set up, adding nutrition for people who grew weak and for those that were recovering, but it was very limited because of insufficient supplies. A mandatory bath and steam were held every two weeks against lice and undergarments had to be washed once a weak.

Workshops were set up where tailors and shoemakers had to manufacture uniforms for the workers.

Under these conditions, the winter of 1943-44 passed by very quickly. Debates focused on politics and work. There were those who were discussing the general situation, others were sharing the events at work, such as how someone who was a few minutes late received 20 flogs as punishment and how someone else, who did not comply with the quota the Germans demanded, was badly beaten. The manager in one of the sections, after receiving bad news from home, was beating and torturing Jews. In another section, as a punishment for something, they had to work 18 hours a day.

Another search was conducted in the barracks after several people from the factory escaped. The Germans were thinking of dyeing our clothes, but they were eventually satisfied with a general headcount. They assigned each worker with a Star of David and a number, engraved on a square can. We had to carry these numbers at all times, and if the Germans found someone without his number, they would shave off his hair as punishment.

Part Two

One day, Lasinski's wife came to Hasag, sparking concerns that something bad was about to happen. A general assembly was called for the next day and we were restless and afraid. Was another selection or some *sort of shipment to be announced? In the end, it turned out to be just another headcount.*

Several days later, at the guard commander's order, a group of Jewish firefighters was formed; at first, it was made up of 10 men, but with time, their numbers and scope of activity grew. And so, we witnessed drills by the Jewish firefighters, whose members were wearing red bands with the words Juedische Fuercshutz *(Jewish fire fighters) inscribed on them. Afterward, the group's members received firefighter shirts and their deployment positions.*

One day, 30 carpenters had to go to the Varta factory—it was being transferred to Hasag and was about to become an ammunition workshop, and the carpenters were told to prepare rooms for the Jews that were to arrive there. The firefighters were told to lead those Jews, because no one wanted to go there. They followed the order and returned after several weeks with about 300 Jews from Plashov, a concentration camp near Krakow. They told us that there were still about 12,000 Jews living in Plashov toward the end of 1943, but hundreds were dying there every day after being tortured and murdered by the Germans, with the help of the Jewish police. Some of these cops came to the Varta factory, but their attitude toward their Jewish brothers remained unchanged.

Here, in Pelzery, no fireman or work manager would allow himself to do to Jews the things that the Jewish cops did in Varta. When a Jewish cop came to Pelzery, the only reason that he was not beaten up was because he was escorted by the camp's guards. Even the firemen found it hard to stop the raging crowd and protect him, for among the Częstochowa youth the spirit of the ghetto was still alive and kicking, and the members of the resistance groups bound together from the very first moment.

Groups, sometimes numbering 20 people, sometimes smaller, would gather in the corner. They somehow smuggled some money from the ghetto and decided to buy bread with it every day. We were getting a coupon for 15 lunches from the Interior Service every day. That way, we managed the food while at the same time making sure we did not look too cheery. We had to trust our strength in the camp. Some of the people thought that we were the reason the camp was closed.

We had contact only with Rakow. The people there informed us of the disaster that struck our post in Kolonia. We were also told that our post was maintaining contact with Warsaw, from where we were hoping help would arrive. And help was coming: Mediated by our friends in the Rakow factory, we received certain sums of money that were divided between the members of the resistance group. To us, it was not mere material aid, but also proof that there were still people out there in the world who remembered us and though about us. We were working and suffering, but it was made easier for us, knowing that someone cared about us.

Meanwhile, no political steps were being taken on any front to end the war. Winter passed, giving way to spring. *The factory was growing and developing and needed more and more people. The* infanterie *(infantry section) that was producing rifle munitions was expanding. There were rumors that Jews from* Litzmannstadt *(Łódź) were coming and indeed, about 1,000 people from the Łódź Ghetto came to Częstochowa. Five hundred of them ended up in Peltzery, 300 in Varta and 200 reached Częstochowska, where the Germans were planning to build a car engine factory. This factory belonged to the Herman Gering factory.*

The Jews from Łódź were very thin and exhausted, but they were all dressed well. They were starving, which was not surprising, since food allocations in the ghetto were meager and buying food privately was very expensive: two kilograms of bread cost about 1,000 Deutsche Marks. The people from Łódź told us that there were still 70,000 Jews living in the Łódź Ghetto and that there were even many cases of childbirth.

The Łódź people were not housed in the barracks. The men were living in the "Circus," and the women in what was called "Rakow Hall," outside the shed area. To distinguish them from the others, they were made to wear white arm bands with their numbers, like other Jews that were living outside the ghetto. The Jews that were allowed to exit for Kolonia were made to wear green arm bands with their numbers and that way almost every group had a number that was marked differently.

When we tried talking to the Łódź people about the war and what we were going through, and told them about Treblinka and the annihilation of the Jewish people, they refused to believe us. They simply could not grasp that something like that was possible and no amount of proof could convince them otherwise. They were very optimistic and they were sure that they would survive. They did not believe in the possibility of our annihilation.

They changed their mind soon enough, though, when they witnessed the German's cruelty firsthand. They saw people beaten brutally for no reason, saw how people were led to the guardroom and rarely emerged, or how during a search that was conducted on one of the workers, the Germans found a letter to a Pole and the Gestapo arrested both him and his wife—neither of whom were heard of again. Such incidents were part of the daily routine. The Łódź people were sometimes victims of their own carelessness, taking risks by selling clothes to Poles and sometimes caught by the guard factories while buying bread. After they came, bread prices rose and a shortage ensued, but it was short and prices soon went back to normal.

The month of May arrived and a different mood took a hold of us. The living conditions improved slightly and people were talking about nutrient supplements from the Red Cross—for how else could this improvement in the quality of our lunches, and the increase of bread quotas to 500 grams a day be explained? We were also getting a few hundreds grams of sugar, margarine or jam a week; and on several occasions we received cigarettes, so all that improved the general mood. On work-free days, groups of men and women would gather in the barracks and songs, recitations, or monologues could be heard. A Jewish song about suffering, survival and a better tomorrow was created, as were songs about the tragedy of the Jewish people, about the dreams of every Jew, the purpose of our suffering and about vengeance. Late at night, a sad and touching Jewish song or a heart-wrenching recitation, full of pain, could be heard.

Sometimes, the factory guards and Germans would join us on these nights and then the atmosphere would change and became lighter. The Germans, for their part, tried to amuse us by organizing ball games. A team was formed in each of the factory divisions and games were held several times a week. They caught the attention of many and even the German foremen showed great interest. One could have thought that the invasion had begun.

The world was reaching a boiling point and the Germans wanted to divert everyone's attention from political issues, but not everyone was interested in ball games. People from the resistance group found out that letters were sent to us from leading Jewish figures in Warsaw, who said that they remembered us and were doing everything they could on our behalf. They sent us a booklet called "A Year in Treblinka" and after reading it, we could not think of games anymore. They told us that we needed to organize a mass escape.

We believed that the invasion would be the last phase of the war, that the decision about our fate was *approaching and that we had to be alert. At that time, letters and formal postcards from Łódź were arriving, but since they were all censured, nothing special was written in them. We could have replied from Częstochowa, but only in so many words.*

The days were passing by, one resembling the next. The operations in France were advancing very slowly. One night, news came of an assassination attempt against Hitler. It was 1 a.m. and people came running from the factory to the barracks with the news that Hitler was giving a radio speech during which sounds of explosions were heard. After several minutes, it was reported that there was an attempt on the Führer's life—a bomb was thrown at him. People were overjoyed and no one could sleep. People were constantly arriving from the factory with more news. The foremen were not in the halls, there was chaos everywhere and the camp guards were nowhere in sight. Joy, ah, the madness of joy. Could liberation be near? Maybe this was the moment we were all waiting for for such a long time? Even if the war was not over, if there was only a different government in Germany, maybe then our lives would be worth something. Maybe this night would bring a different morning, a better one? Maybe tomorrow would smile on us.

This went on for several hours, after which the foremen returned to the factory halls and the camp guards chased all the people back inside the barracks. But something was hanging in the air. The foremen were walking around unsure and confused, disquiet visible on their faces. Occasionally, they would leave work to listen to the latest news. The Jews assembled in groups, passing the fresh news around. One foreman had gone to the casino again, where they had a radio transmitter, to hear the latest news. Another asked him what was new and apparently, Hitler was severely wounded, some members of his entourage were killed, there were riots in Berlin and a new government was giving orders.

It was 7 a.m. The Poles came to work and brought a newspaper, announcing that the assassination attempt against Hitler had failed. The Führer was wounded but alive and Himmler was now in command. The Nazis were firmly in control of the situation. Our happiness was premature.

There was more news the next day. Hitler published a pamphlet, ordering people to disregard the traitors who were giving orders on his behalf. Changes were made in high-ranking military positions. The situation was still unclear, but we were still fostering some illusions. Over the next few days, we learned of the deaths of more than 10 German generals and of multiple arrests among the senior officers. The revolt failed and everything was getting back to normal. We were working, suffering, and waiting. After work, soccer games became the highlight of our day.

One event stayed with us for several days: L. Fux, A former member of the Internal Jewish Service and an informant, had died. In one of his reports, he had implicated a commander of the guards and the latter promised Fux that he would get even. When Fux died, the commander organized a funeral for him, which I want to describe here.

The body was put on a matrass and carried to the cemetery accompanied by 30 Jews and the werkschutz unit, with their commander in the lead. They ordered the Jews to dig a hole and placed the dead inside in a seated position. The commander of the guards fired a series of shots at the body from an automatic weapon and then every werkschutz officer shot the dead body in the head. Each of the Jews was then made to throw a stone at the body. Some were made to sing while others were forced to cover the grave with stones. Some Jews were ordered to dance on the grave. This ceremony lasted for more than an hour. That evening, at the commander of the guards' demand, a concert was held in the barracks area to "properly honor the memory of the rat."

The Soviet attack had begun and we were curiously following its progress, as it was reportedly going well. Vilna was liberated. A few days later Brest, Lvov, and Bialystok were liberated as well. After Brest, the Soviets moved to Lublin and a few days later the city was liberated.

People in the factory were filled with excitement, thinking that if things would continue this way the Russians would reach us within two weeks. Dęblin was liberated. The Bolsheviks crossed the Wisła River and were marching from Bialystok and Lublin toward

Warsaw. *What will become of us? Will they send us deeper into Germany? Some believed so. Others, with a more pessimistic view, said that we would be murdered here. Men from the resistance group started to organize self-defense measures in case that happens. The possibilities were slim, but those that existed were used to their full potential.*

The Russian military's progress continued and the Red Army was said to be about 60 kilometers from Skarzysko. The Germans were evacuating Skarzysko and trains loaded with machines and different materials kept arriving from that direction. They said that the area's Jews would be arriving, too. The movements in the factory yard and in the markets were fervent. Trucks were arriving full, leaving their cargo, and turning around to bring a new one. The wives of the German foremen were packing and the carpenters were busy making wooden crates for the Germans.

They said that there were already several hundred Jews that arrived to Varta from Skarzysko and that they were about to arrive here any day now. Barracks were prepared for them. A few thousand arrived by train, heavily escorted by the military police, dirty, miserable people, wearing rags, some of whom were staying in our factory, Peltzery. Others went to Varta and the rest to Rakow. Some groups were taken elsewhere, probably to Lipsk. Upon their arrival, the disorder in the factory grew. People had nothing to do so the Germans ordered three, eight-hour shifts in the different factories.

A new kitchen was set up. Foremen from Skarzysko also arrived—some stayed, some continued on.

News from Rakow, through which a train to Kielce was passing, had arrived. We were told that transports of Jews from different camps were passing through Kielce every day. Those trains were headed to Auschwitz.

Rakow was in panic. One night, during an aerial raid, 20 people escaped. A week later, eight more escaped. In Peltzery, people were starting to consider doing the same. The front line was growing near and the Germans were starting to dig trenches around Częstochowa.

We had escaped in groups of three, but we still maintained contact with the factory. The Germans did not respond to our escape, but it seemed as if they had a premonition that something was about to happen. A search was conducted in the barracks, and knives, hammers and similar objects were seized. About a week later, they reinstated 12-hour shifts again. One section, Geschoss (Shells), was transferred, people and machines alike, to the Varta factory. Two more people escaped. The Soviet attack came to a halt, but war was raging in on France. It was better for us—we preferred that the war end far away from us, in Western Europe, so when the day of Germany's surrender arrives, they would each think of themselves and we would be able to survive somehow. That was what most people thought would happen and the mood had improved. We hoped the eastern front would hold for as long as possible so that the British could advance.

The Germans had lost their confidence and were meeting the factory's orders as necessary. They were needed bakers and about 30 Jewish bakers from Peltzery virtually took over the bakeries in the city. Each morning, they were escorted to work by a factory guard and were also brought back by one. Their situation was pretty good.

One day, a siren sounded in the factory. Lavor, one of the factory lines where shells were filled with gunpowder and the bullets were assembled, was on fire. A crate of gunpowder caught fire and Lavor burnt down. If the wind had shifted the fire would have reached the gunpowder warehouse and the entire factory would have exploded. The firefighter's immediate response extinguished the fire. No one was killed and only a few people suffered some burns.

The Hasag from Kielce was evacuated and transferred to Częstochowska. Some of the people from Peltzery were ordered to go there as well.

The newspapers brought good news that was only getting better: The allies landed in the south of France; Romania surrendered; Paris was liberated; Finland was seeking a truce; Bulgaria sought an alliance with the Soviets and the government in Hungary resigned. In Slovakia, the military joined the communist uprising; the Balkans were in flames; France was now almost entirely free of Germans; the allies had parachuted into Holland successfully and the British were standing on German soil.

Our chances of survival were increasing every day. Maybe now Germany was going to break. We were waiting. We were ready to die, and awaiting our liberation.

These words ended the notes in my brother's notebook. Yehiel-Heniek Wodzislawski's, R.I.P.

The Hell of a Bunker Resident:
My Mother's Ordeals

The house we lived in was on a street that was included in the first deportation aktzia, in September 1942, a day after Yom Kippur. The metallurgical factory, where those who were selected and were eligible to work and were about to stay, was on the same street. When I left with my brother for the metallurgical factory, we agreed that our parents were not going to become a part of the aktzia under any circumstances and that they will try to hide somehow.

Unfortunately, my father—who remained an optimist from the beginning of the war—believed the Germans promises and when the military police came to banish the last remaining residents from their homes, he was the first one to step outside into the street.

My mother, with her sharp intuition, retreated toward the yard that was behind the house. She was unable to leave us—she could not think about the possibility of life without her children—and she was completely aware of her actions, of their implications and of the hardships she would now face. But her goal was clear: she would remain at her children's side at all cost and will always protect them, wherever they go.

She noticed that some of the building's residents, joined by their relatives, had also turned to the back-yard. Once she approached it, she had no doubt that there was a bunker in the yard, and not just one, but two. This was the height of initiative and innovation, combined with the utmost secrecy: to dig two large bunkers and somehow keep all the neighbors and even the landlord, who visited often, completely oblivious to it. No one noticed a thing.

It was very late when my mother entered the yard and everyone was already sitting in the bunker; but there was just enough time to remove the lid, descend to the bunker, and replace it, so no one was the wiser.

The bunker my mother came down to was very large. There were more than 30 people there, as well as an entire warehouse of different goods and materials, mainly new textiles. Three heavily secured portholes allowed some weak light inside.

As it turned out, it was not the only bunker. Another bunker, dug in a different part of the yard housed 10-12 people, whose job was to cover the entrance to the big bunker.

Less than five minutes after my mother's arrival, the Ukrainians and Germans began searching the yard.

Suddenly, shouts were heard from a nearby summer-house. Several young people were trying to hide there from the aktzia, but the Germans had plenty of experience and knew how to conduct a thorough search. After prolonged beseeching, the Germans opted not to kill the Jews, sending them to the collection point instead. A few minutes later, everything calmed down, but gunshots could be heard from a distance.

There were also children in the bunker, sitting calmly and quietly, understanding—or rather sensing—the dread of the situation. They already knew what hiding underground meant. There was silence in the bunker. Everyone was preoccupied with their own thoughts, worrying about the fate of their relatives. No one thought about food—no one was hungry. The gravity inside the bunker was immense and there was a shortage of air. People were huddled inside the bunker and thirst was prevalent. The situation grew worse with time, but no one complained. People were accustomed to suffering in silence. Only their faces expressed the great tension, their eyes surrounded by dark circles. Suddenly, a sob was heard from the corner. One of the women was crying—she did not know where her husband was. No one consoled her. No one uttered a word.

The need to control one's bodily functions proved the most difficult. The adults were able to hold it in, but the children could not. The stench and suffocation increased, but everyone was slowly getting used to it. The will to survive was stronger than anything else.

Things were a little better at night. The lid was removed, and several brave people went outside. The people in the other bunker did the same. Whispers could be heard at night—people were sharing their experiences, giving each other advice. Suddenly, a gunshot was heard nearby. Everyone ran back to their bunkers immediately. All was silent again. One of the men went out to bring water from the well. A mild shaking sound was heard and the bucket sank down and brought up water. The dense liquid, infested with tadpoles and frogs, could hardly be called water, but no one paid any attention to that—throats were dry and there was no other choice.

The next day brought with it a beautiful morning. The sun was shining with thousands of colors and its rays tried to reach the people that had buried themselves alive. And what could be seen in that light? Tormented people, who one man had ordered to hate and kill, holding on to hope. They wanted to live to see better days, to witness the defeat of those that swore to kill them. The children, those poor toddlers who never harmed a soul, who knew nothing of evil, why did they have to go through all of this suffering? Why? The civilized world, which was watching in silence as these innocent souls were murdered, should be made to answer that question.

The second day in the bunker was not as nice as the day before. On the contrary, the lack of air and the heat grew worse. Sweat was pouring down people's faces and bodies seemed paralyzed. It was the second day that no one had eaten a thing. No one was feeling hungry.

My mother decided to move to the Barland factory

during the night. The factory belonged to the Landau brothers and bordered the yard. The move was easy because there were two big holes in the fence separating the two. There were two large trenches where 150 people, with their children and possessions, were hiding. There were alcoves in the trenches' walls, where people were lying down. The smell of decay and human excretions was in the air. My mother came across many acquaintances there, including her brother. Unlike the bunker, they were disorganized. Hesitant conversations could be heard and sometimes someone's silent cry, or a sigh.

A grown man was seen in the candle light, praying fervently and beating his chest. Blessed be the man who believes and accepts God's decisions with the humility of a monk. The situation was worse for the youth, who were crammed inside the condensed walls of the trenches. Their souls were tortured: they were vibrant and rebellious and the will to live was vital inside them. But it was too late. By the time people understood the situation they were in, it was too late.

In the meantime, hunger was becoming a serious issue. The supplies were gone and people realized that they now had to come up with ways of getting food, because it was clear that they would have to stay in hiding for a very long time. The youth took this mission upon themselves: at night, they would sneak outside the bunker very carefully—because Ukrainians and military policemen from the security service at the metallurgical factory were constantly roaming around—and bring food from nearby houses. Complete silence had to be kept during the day because oftentimes, military officers would come to the factory. What for? No one knew at the time.

Inside the trenches, the situation was worsening. One of the women had lost her senses and was yelling incessantly. No one was able to calm her down and there was a risk that her voice would give away the location of the people in the bunker. Therefore, my mother decided to leave that place and return to the building where her apartment was, which was standing empty, and hide in one of its attics during the days of the aktzia. Others followed her, most of them our neighbors. They settled in the attic too, where hiding was easiest. They brought sheets to cover the floor and utensils for cooking. The water shortage was the most difficult to bear. Supplies to the ghetto were terminated, to force those who were in hiding to come out. With great difficulty and in the cover of night, they were able to achieve the valuable liquid from the well in the yard.

Life in the attic was much easier than in the trenches but it was more dangerous, too. The steps of the guards passing by the wide-open gate were constantly heard, but people were still walking around the apartments in search of food. The vigilance that was kept so diligently at first was now abandoned and reminders and pleas did not help. There were those—especially those who collected valuables left in the abandoned apartments—who were careless and could bring about the disclosure of the hiding place. One day, the thing they dreaded the most transpired: two people from the bunker in the yard came to the building to take some food. On their way back, they were spotted by a German military police patrol that was passing by. The Jews started to run, but the Germans' bullets caught up with them and they were shot to death.

All of a sudden, a terrible cry was heard. The wife of one of the murdered men witnessed his death from her hiding place and could not contain her grief. Her cries grew stronger and turned into a wail of despair. The German sadist smiled with satisfaction—the scream intoxicated him, as if it was beautiful music to his ears that sounded every day. An aktzia was immediately put in motion. The military officers came running over at the sound of the gunshots and started searching the nearby apartments and pantries. Time after time, they pulled someone out and made them stand with the rest of the people in the yard. A fairly large group was assembled. Miraculously, the Germans did not search the attic, where everyone froze in place, afraid that the slightest noise would lead to their discovery.

My mother was in the basement when this transpired, and the entire spectacle took place right before her very eyes. What did she feel when she saw the people she was hiding with for so long being led to their deaths? She became enraged by the Germans' actions as well as with those who were across the ocean, seemingly oblivious to the mass, merciless murder of their brethren.

Everybody knew that the entire building would be searched within a few hours. The people that were hiding in the attic decided to leave it and snuck back to the Barland factory. Only one woman decided to stay behind and hide in the building, because she did not believe the Germans and she did not want to go to Barland with everyone else. My mother, it seems was guided by a sixth sense: Since she predicted that the building would be thoroughly searched, she knew she had to hide in a place no one would think of looking in. She chose to hide in a very small and dark basement with no windows, where she brought rags and junk from other basements and hid under them.

Her assumptions turned out to be correct: within a few hours, a large group of Ukrainians with a few Gestapo officers had arrived in the neighborhood and a raid ensued. From basements to attics, they left no stone unturned. Every corner, pantry, and crevice was checked.

The Germans were not satisfied with just that and were also banging on walls and floorboards to make sure that they were no hidden hiding places. A Ukrainian with a flashlight in his hand was walking on the pile my mother was lying under.

This went on for hours. When she met up with my brother and me later, my mother told us that in those moments she was wondering if it was worth it, to suffer so much, to fight so desperately for such a miserable life. But then her maternal instinct awoke and the will to see her children gave her strength.

It was now a new time in my mother's life: she had to fend for herself, get her own food and water, and look out for her own safety. It was as silent as a tomb inside the house, a silence that was worse than any other noise. After the Germans left, the building looked as if it had been through a pogrom. The doors to all the apartments were broken, rags and various effects were scattered around, closets and drawers were ripped open and signs of looting and plunder were everywhere.

My mother was in her apartment, near the attic, where she made herself a hideout. To save herself from going hungry, she would knead dough during the day and at night, in the moonlight, she would light a fire and bake bread. The smoke that was coming out of the chimney, which could have revealed her location, could not be seen at night. She covered the window with a blanket to make sure the light of the fire remained unseen.

One night, my mother's brother came over from Barland and asked her to move there with them. But my mother refused. She did not believe the Germans would allow people they had no use for live. Her prophecies were fulfilled, unfortunately. The next day, she heard a commotion near the gate. Captain Degenhart was holding a selection in Barland. All those who just a short while ago were able to hide in the bunker and escape the Germans were apprehended. Out of the 2,000 people that were in Barland, only 30 remained. Suddenly, footsteps were heard in the yard. One of the people who was designated for shipment escaped the factory and hid in the building. My mother called him over and he told her what had happened outside. He stayed with her all day and at night, after dinner, he refused to listen to her pleas to stay inside and went out, intending to cross over to the Aryan side. No one knows whether he succeeded.

About two weeks after the aktzia began, I found my mother and was able to keep in touch with her after that. Our meeting was completely coincidental and this is how it happened: The Barland factory was near our house. On the first day of the aktzia, when my brother and I left the house, we passed through the metallurgical factory first, because our cards were in order. A week later, after the commissioner of the Horowitz and Barland factories came to take workers and the locksmiths, we ended up in that group. For different reasons we were better off there, but most importantly, we were staying in the Horowitz factory, which was on the same street we lived on.

We were not being watched, by the Germans or by the Ukrainians, so we could walk around the entire area freely; and since the workers from the Barland factory were also living in Horowitz, I was allowed to go there after a week as well. As the Barland factory bordered our house, I had a feeling that despite the aktzias, one of my parents was alive and in hiding and I decided to go look for them.

It was a cloudy October Saturday and we went out to work in the Barland factory. I took a bag with some pieces of bread in it, which my brother and I had managed to get. Carefully and quietly, I moved from the factory to the yard and I found a small bunker inside it that was empty. I continued searching and after a few minutes, I came to the empty building. I made quick work of checking all of the basements and attics, but I could not find any signs of life. The place was empty and silent as a tomb. Only the wind made the windows rattle from time to time. I was filled with tremendous despair and sorrow. I had so much hope for that journey! Pain pierced my heart and tears were running down my cheeks.

I decided to search the apartment where my family used to live one last time. I climbed upstairs and tried to mute my steps so they could barely be heard. I walked into the apartment and met the same chaos as in the other flats, when my mother suddenly came out of her hiding place. Was she a ghost? A figment of my imagination? I could not believe my eyes or the sight of my hands hugging the person I loved the most. My father, unfortunately, was gone. He went with everyone else. He did not want to listen to my mother, who pleaded him to stay in hiding with her.

I decided to stay with my mother and get through the raids and aktzias with her, but she strongly objected, saying she would be able to hide better alone and that if I stayed, the thought of the danger I would be placing myself in alone would unsettle her. After many pleas and much begging, I had no other choice but to agree. She did not want to accept the bread I brought with me and to appease me she showed me the bread she had baked herself. The only thing she was missing was water. The hours passed by quickly. It was hard for me to leave my mother, but when it was dark, I had to return and join the group that was going to Horowitz at night.

A selection process took place the next day. It took place on a Sunday, when no one expected it. In the morning, news came that Degenhart had gone to a nearby town to conduct an aktzia against the Jews there. The people in the bunkers allowed themselves to step outside and walk around. All of a sudden, at 10 a.m. Captain Rohn showed up—he was Degenhart's right-hand man and one of the greatest sadists there—and together with a military police officer he ordered everyone to assemble right away. He threatened us that if we did not come out, he would have the Ukrainians search the entire factory area.

Those who were in the yard were arrested immediately. The elderly were removed from the line and sent to the aktzia gathering point. But Rohn was not satisfied with that. He suspected there were others in hiding and demanded that everyone come out. When he saw that people were not complying, he declared that he was going to come back with the Ukrainians in the afternoon and conduct a thorough search. Panic ensued once he left and anxiety and constant movement took over. Everyone, according to their ability, hid in different places, waiting to see what the next few hours would bring.

Rohn was punctual: several minutes before three o'clock in the afternoon, he returned with two Ukrainians and a few non-commissioned officers from the military police in tow. They were experts in finding people and so a manhunt began. In the meantime, Rohn was scanning all the people who were part of the work staff and were standing in the plaza. Those he did not like were set aside. He ordered Horowitz, the factory's owner, to tell him where people were hiding. Horowitz refused and claimed he did not know, so one of the Germans started hitting him over the head with a club.

Meanwhile, the search party was producing more and more people, found in various hiding places. One of the military officers was running around with a gun in his hand, sniffing the air and searching like a dog. A rather large group of people was standing on one side, meant to go to the aktzia. Those who remained included their brothers, sisters, sons and daughters, who were standing and watching how the people closest to them were being taken for extermination. They were trying to control their shivering. There was nothing they could do to help, but they could ask to join the deported—the

Germans agreed to that. A young woman asked Rohn to let her stay without the boy and the boy, as though understanding what was going on, hugged her and put his head on her. The German was unfazed and the Ukrainians, using the butts of their rifles, pushed the mother and her child toward the line.

Several dozen people were still able to hide in various places. I came to visit my mother the next day, using the same way I did the last time, and when I came in I saw great fear in her eyes. It turned out that a moment before my arrival there was a Ukrainian in the building, walking between the apartments. My mother did not have time to hide in the attic, so she locked the apartment door. The Ukrainian passed through all the apartments and when he found the locked door he started pounding on it with force. When that did not help, he tried breaking it down. Fortunately, the door was strong and so was the lock. He went away angry, cursing at the world.

My mother feared not only for herself, but for me as well, because she knew I was on my way. If I had met the Ukrainian, my life would not have been worth a dime. But despite everything, I continued to visit the empty and haunted house twice a day over the next few days, to be with her. Her pleas and explanations did not help—my love for my mother overcame all the obstacles. Every time I came over, I brought some warm food from the factory and any other food products I obtained.

As time went by, we were facing greater hardships and increasing danger. Polish workers came to the factory and they continuously plundered everything that still remained in nearby buildings after the Jews were deported. One night, my mother heard quiet steps on the stairwell and immediately locked the door. After a moment, two civilians with bags on their backs came upstairs. After they had collected loot from nearby apartments, the thieves started to approach the door behind which my mother was standing. They decided to break it down, hoping that someone was hiding there and they would be able to get a hefty bribe in exchange for their silence. From their conversation, which my mother heard from behind the door, she could be facing the worse possible outcome, because she had nothing to bribe them with. Her blood froze in her veins. The door squeaked when the two robbers pushed it with their shoulders and suddenly gunfire was heard from behind the door. A drunken Ukrainian was shooting at the door for amusement. How ironic, that this person, who had tortured and murdered Jews, had—unbeknown to him—saved one of them. The thieves heard the gunshot and ran away. Once again, luck saved my mother's life.

The Germans, meanwhile, were organizing the ghetto's "cleansing": They started their project on the streets from which the deportation began and chose special work groups that were comprised of Jews for this task; therefore creating the need to hide from those that came to "cleanse." The danger was significant, since the Jewish workers were accompanied by Polish policemen and German military officers, who wanted to make sure the Jews would not steal anything. We decided that my mother would hide in the pantry, which she did that very night, taking food and other essential items with her. While she was hiding in the pantry, she risked visits by these goons, who treated Jews with much hostility, and did not hesitate to hand them over to the Germans.

After "cleansing" the apartments, the workers turned their attention to the pantries and basements, which forced my mother to leave her hiding place and find a better one. She decided to hide in the bunker in the yard, the one that had not been discovered at that time. At night, when it was quiet, my mother moved to her new hiding place, taking some essential things with her. With a heavy heart and a somber thought, she went down to that "grave." My brother and I gave her food and water through the ventilation holes. My mother had a bad feeling sitting in that basement, alone in the dark, in the stale air, filled with uncertainty.

Two days, which seemed like eternity, passed between my mother's decision to enter the bunker in the yard and the time when she was discovered. Jewish workers, who under the Germans' orders were searching for bunkers, came across her hiding place. They were taken aback, shouting in fear and surprise at the sight of the slender woman, who had managed to stay alive after so many days of aktzia. My mother realized that if she wanted to stay alive she had to escape as fast as she could. Once the workers saw her, they ran to the military officer to report it, but when they came back with the military officer they found that the basement was empty! The officer was furious. He cursed, upset that such a treat—another Jew for him to kill—had managed to escape from right under his nose.

My mother knew that the only way for her to save herself was to get to the Barland factory and enter its bathroom. The move was not difficult, because the yard boarded the factory and there was a big hole in the fence. The only obstacle was the soft ground where her footprints remained. But my mother had a solution for that too: she went to the other yard and left footprints pointing in the opposite direction, then she came back and went through the hole in the factory fence and hid in the bathroom. This entire journey lasted less than two minutes.

The military officer ordered a search of every corner of the yard and threatened the two Jews that if they did not find the woman, they will be shot. But despite their thorough search and their attempt to guess where she had escaped to, they could not track her down. After half an hour of searching, the officer ordered them to stop. He claimed that it was impossible that the woman had managed to escape in such a short amount of time without their help and cocked his weapon, ready to kill them.

Meanwhile, the incident was reported to the German

headquarters and Degenhart arrived at the yard with his entourage. He was amazed to learn the facts and demanded to know how any woman could last for so long on her own. No one had an answer to that question. For some reason, the Germans decided to spare the lives of the Jews that discovered the bunker, but not before they received a decent beating and were made to kneel in the yard, in the pouring rain for hours. Wagons were brought in after that to carry away the goods that were found in the bunker.

My mother, who was fearfully hiding in the factory bathroom, watched what was going on through the window with a trembling heart. Her strength had forsaken her, she was consumed by doubt, and she did not want to live anymore. She regretted having the urge to be saved. But then, like in previous moments of despair, she thought of her children—she was willing to fight for them like a lioness, until her last breath. These thoughts gave her the courage she needed.

Meanwhile, the Barland factory was rife with rumors about what was happening on the other side of the fence. One of the workers approached my brother and told him that a woman was supposedly hiding in the bathroom. My brother, who had a feeling that it was our mother, immediately ran over there. It was a dangerous move since a military policeman was patrolling the yard and on the other side of the fence, the factory's Polish workers and clerks were hostile to Jews.

There was only one place to hide inside the

factory—the water tower. But during the day it was impossible to get there without attracting the workers' attention. Hiding in the water tower could also end badly at any moment, but there was little choice and my mother had to stay inside the bathroom all day and sneak into the tower at night.

It was the worst day in a series of bad days my mother had experienced until then. The foreman, who was informed that a strange woman was inside the bathroom, went in to check. And again, it was one of those times when my mother's luck played in her favor and he did not peep inside the stall she was in. What discouraged him—we'll never know, but it was possible he did it on purpose, for he was a discrete man.

The day passed in constant anxiety and fear. Every German that came to the factory that day was another reason for concern. Anxious, we followed as the events in the yard unfolded. The day grew endlessly long. We were looking forward to the relief that sundown would bring. At night, silence took over the factory. Only in the yard, where the bunker was, movement could be felt—the Jewish workers were emptying the bunker of all the things found in it. It prevented us from transferring our mother to the water tower at sunset, as we planned.

Around midnight everything became still. There was complete darkness and even the moon could not be seen. It was time to move mother to her new hiding place. There was no ladder there, only steps bolted onto the wall and a completely physically and emotionally exhausted woman had to climb those metal steps. But when a person has a goal, he fights for it. At that moment, our mother's goal was to stay alive; to survive, to be with her children.

My mother stayed in the tower. The primary mission—and the most difficult one—was bringing her food. It had to be done in a way that no one would notice and tell the Germans. We eventually managed it, after many efforts, but even staying in that hideout was complicated. One day, my mother heard someone climbing up. At first, she thought it was one of us, bringing her food, but then she was terrified to realize that it was a stranger who was climbing the iron steps. She immediately hid under a pile of rags and garbage. As it turned out, one of the Polish workers hid some items he had stolen from nearby houses up there and had now come to collect them. He was stunned to find a stranger woman living in such conditions. My mother had to quickly make up an excuse that will somehow justify her being in the tower. Since she spoke Polish well and did not have a "Semitic look," she presented herself as a Pole who came at night to take some of what was left by the Jews for herself, but had the bad luck of being seen by the Germans. She escaped in the dark, she said, and sprained her ankle. Having no other choice, she was hiding up there for now.

The worker immediately left her alone, but he demanded the wedding ring my mother had on her finger, as a price for his silence. Seeing that could save her from the Germans, she gave him the ring without any hesitation. He took the bribe and then said he would come back the next day and bring her some food.

Meanwhile, the Jews that remained in the ghetto after the shipments had started were trying to adapt to their new living conditions. It was not easy, since family life could not be maintained. Only remnants of families were left, everyone was alone, or with a sibling at best, and raids meant to capture children and the elderly were still conducted by the Germans.

That is why my mother did not return to the ghetto. We were afraid for her, mainly because it was still very unsafe in the small ghetto. My brother and I were living in the Horowitz factory then, which was subjected to the whims of the same German commissioner who also controlled the Barland factory.

Soon after that, our situation changed and we had to move to the small ghetto. We decided we had to take our mother with us—she could no longer stay in the tower and she had to leave that hideout immediately. We took advantage of an opportunity that arose when we were sent to the ghetto on an errand, under the supervision of a policeman who was working for both factories. Inside the ghetto, we asked some acquaintances to take our mother in for a few days, until we moved to the ghetto. A few hours later, at dusk, the same officer moved our mother to the small ghetto. My brother accompanied them.

That is how the first part of the struggle waged by this heroic woman, who stood against the murderers with such vigor and courage and at a great personal cost, came to its end.

I will never forget my mother's short period of terror; I will never forget her face, her eyes. Mother! The things you did for your children will stay not only in their memories, but also in their hearts; rooted deeply as a monument to your pain and suffering, your love and your courage.

***

I do not know how my mother died. The last time I saw her was in June 1943, when the small ghetto in Częstochowa was liquidated. Everyone had to be at a set place and the Germans announced that whoever failed to come out would be shot on sight. My mother did not come out.

A month after the liquidation of the small ghetto, something that is hard to explain happened to my brother and me: We were both in Hasag factories and I had a strange dream one night and in the morning I told my brother: "Heniek, I dreamed that mother was alive." Heniek looked at me with a strange look on his face and said, "I dreamed the same thing last night."

***

I wrote about the rest of my experiences during World War II many years ago, right after my liberation, when I started to write down my memoires.

After the liquidation of the small ghetto, Heniek and I found ourselves in the Hasag camp. Hasag was an abbreviation of the German names "Hugo Schneider Co. AG." This association had several branches in Poland as well as in other countries the Germans had conquered. The factory we were working in was called Peltzery, and it was one of the largest textile plants in Częstochowa. Sometime after taking Częstochowa, the Germans turned this plant into an ammunition factory. They brought in the necessary equipment from Germany and the workforce was made up of Poles and Jews. The Jews made up the majority of the workforce, as they were forced to work for free. The factory's management was in German hands and they supervised the work and the foremen.

Thousands of Jews were working in these factories. Until June 1943, many Jews from the small ghetto were taken for labor in Hasag. They would leave in the morning and come back to the ghetto at night.

The small ghetto was what all that was left of the big ghetto and its 40,000 Jews. After the murderous aktzias and the shipments to the Treblinka death camp, some 5,000 people remained in the small ghetto. They were all working in different German stations in and around the city of Częstochowa, but the largest group of Jews from the small ghetto was working in Hasag. My brother and I worked in the Landau factory first, which also manufactured weapon parts for the German Army. There were almost no Germans in this factory at all.

We realized that the small ghetto was being liquidated and that it was just a matter of time before the Germans did the same with us. My brother Heniek and I considered how we could avoid the same fate as our relatives and the rest of Hitler's victims. One possibility was escaping into the forest, which entailed great difficulties and danger.

To be able to make this dream come true we had to be in possession of some kind of weapon. Heniek contacted a Pole who promised he would sell him a small gun. It was very risky, because we did not know that man, who could have betrayed us to the Gestapo; but on the scheduled day, my brother had made the deal. For what was a very large sum of money in those days, he received a small gun but no ammunition, which he promised to bring us in a short while. We had a weapon but we were unable to use it because the man never supplied us with the bullets.

After the Warsaw ghetto uprising in April 1943, the Germans decided to raze all of the small ghettoes and transfer the Jews to death camps, concentration camps and forced labor camps. It happened in Częstochowa on June 26, 1943.

That day, we all stood in the yard in front of the entrance to the ghetto. German officers armed with automatic weapons, as well as Polish and Ukrainian police officers surrounded us. Suddenly, a car arrived and three Germans in civilian clothes, probably Gestapo members, came out with clubs in their hands. One of them pulled out a list and started reading names off it— those were people from the underground and none of them stepped forward. The Gestapo officers had to pass between the lines and pull them out. I will never forget this selection. An officer stood in front of me, looked me in the eyes, moved on and pulled out the guy standing next to me. Everyone who was removed from the lines was made to stand in the center of the yard. After a few minutes, two trucks came and they were ordered to get inside.

More cars carrying Germans with automatic weapons came after a while. As the cars were approaching the nearby street, all the men turned to us and yelled in Yiddish *Nakuma* (revenge) and Shema Israel. They knew where they were heading. They had no doubt it was their last trip.

Why didn't they do something to save themselves? I think they knew that for every desperate act they would do there in the yard, the Nazis would harm the other innocent people standing there.

The residents of the small ghetto were assembled in two places: some 4,500 people were in Hasag and 500 people were in Rakow. Heniek and I found ourselves in

Hasag. The conditions were the same as in the camp: we were living in barracks and sleeping on wooden bunks, with nothing to cover ourselves.

The sanitary conditions were horrible. We did not even have the most basic products to keep clean, we were infested with lice, and it bothered us to no end. We had nothing, nothing at all, except for what we were wearing when we were caught. At work, terror reigned. Our department had two German foremen. The head manager was a man called Gunter, and he would occasionally kick or slap us if he did not like something; and his deputy was a man named Prasse, a cruel brute, who would walk around the halls with a whip he would crack right and left for no apparent reason.

Prasse's wife also worked in Hasag. She was in charge of the Jewish women who were performing quality control over the parts we produced. Every now and again, she would bring a little bread for the Jews without her husband's knowledge, to help them deal with the terrible hunger that gnawed at everyone.

Her husband, for his part, did not miss any opportunity to be cruel to people. I was sent to the guardroom twice, where the Ukrainian werkschutz beat me. Their job was to guard the entire factory and mainly to watch over the Jews. When I was sent to the guardroom, I had to take down my pants and lie on my stomach on a stool. I was hit with a special rubber hose, after which I was unable to sit or lie down.

Prasse sent me to the werkschutz claiming I was

"a terrorist." It was true enough, but I did it in a way so that nothing could be proven. I worked next to the automatic machines that were producing shells, called *geschosse*. This production line required a special mold that was shipped from Germany. These molds would often break and they had to be replaced with new ones. I stole these molds from the warehouse and threw them away. Without these molds, those bullets—the geschosses—could not be made until the molds were replaced.

We were discussing the absurdity that we, the Jews, were making bullets to kill either our brothers or those sent to liberate us.

The work was carried out in 12-hour shifts, day and night. We received 120 grams of bread per day and very little soup, which was water really. The problem was how to obtain more food using different schemes, so we would not collapse at work, to keep us alive, because whoever lost their strength was sent to the extermination camps. Therefore, we had to constantly improvise. Once, Heniek found a pack of used notebooks that we could still get a bucket of soup for in exchange. In order to get food, people would stand next to the heater and a bucket of soup was allotted to a number of people. We used to spill the turbid liquid and on the bottom of the bucket, there was always a potato, whole, or half, which we would eat. Stealing this bucket of soup did not harm a soul—it was only taken from the scraps of food given to the pigs the Germans were breeding for their own needs. The soup was cooked over heaters, the liquid would be poured into buckets and given to the Jews, and the thick potage that was left on the bottom was given to the pigs.

The situation for those who had money was better, for they were able to buy bread from the Poles we worked with. Heniek and I did not have any money, so we had to manage in other ways. For example, Heniek fabricated combs from materials he collected at the foundry. I stole from the carts that used to bring potatoes or potato crumbs. We would later cook them in water and make soup. One day, we found out where they were throwing the empty jam barrels. Together with a friend, we snuck into that yard to scrap for remains. We collected the remains of the jam in a pot and we had something to eat, but we only received jam once a month, so such delicacies were rare.

Once, after I had stolen potato crumbs and my pockets were full, a Ukrainian werkschutz caught me. Since he could not leave his post, he ordered me to stand next to him. My brother and other Jews who saw what was happening offered him money for my release, but he refused—he wanted to hand me over to the commander of the werkschutz and collect an award. I knew that when he would hand me over, I would be ordered to eat soap, which meant certain death. I was indifferent to it and I was not even scared. Death was awaiting me at the hands of the Germans eventually anyway. But that very day, some important inspection committee, which included senior SS and Gestapo officers, was visiting the factory. The guard I was standing next to called his German commander and showed him that my pockets were full of stolen potato crumbs. But the commander was too busy with the inspection committee to pay any attention to me. He grabbed me by the neck, kicked my ass, and told me to go to hell. I was saved!

The Escape

From the moment my brother and I were transferred to the Hasag camp, we knew that we would escape at the first chance we got. Heniek had a Polish friend who used to bring us egg sandwiches twice or three times a week. I remember their taste to this day. This friend had planned that we would escape with his help, but things did not turn out that way. We could only meet with the Poles during work, so we had to consider all the other possibilities for escape. It was complicated, because the camp had a tall fence that was carefully guarded by the werkschutz day and night.

We started investigating the area in order to find a weak spot somewhere. We found it by the tall fence, where we started to pry loose two wooden boards. It took us weeks, because we could only do it during the day, when the werkschutz would step away from it. It was impossible to do at night, because if the guards noticed any movement they would shoot right away.

The question was where would we to go once we escaped. At that time, some Jewish boys who escaped from the small ghetto were staying with the Hajdas family in the town of Secemin, in south-central Poland.

There they organized under the command of Bolek Gewercman. Lucek Frankelberg, my friend from first grade, was with them. The group from Secemin sent Lucek as a contact to the Hasag. We reached an understanding that Heniek and I would escape from the camp with him.

At the beginning of summer in 1944, the Soviet armies reached the banks of the Wisła River. At that time, my brother and I decided that it was time to escape from the camp. The question remained: where should we run to? We knew that Jews were hiding with Gentiles, so we were considering joining the group in Secemin. If the group would prove not to be there, we figured that we would try to get closer to the Wisła River and cross over to the Soviet side on the front line. It was a very hard thing to do, but there was no other choice. There were partisan groups around us, but there were those that would not accept Jews and others were even looking for Jews to kill.

Regardless, we were planning our escape and waiting for the first opportunity to execute it. We knew that certain death awaited us inside the camp and we did not believe that we would live to see the camp's liberation. We had to be careful and make sure that no one found out about our intentions and betray us to the Germans. We guarded the place where we loosened the wooden boards in the fence very carefully. Train tracks ran not far from there, occasionally leading a train to the factory. There was a werkschutz walking along the fence at all times. We approached the fence on several occasions, after the morning census and before we had to report to work, and waited for an opportunity to escape.

One summer Sunday, when we were not far away from the fence, a train suddenly came inside the factory. At that moment, the guard was on the other side of the train, so he could not see us. We used that moment to remove the fence boards and sneak out to the other side. We made it, but then something that we could not have predicted happened: at a distance of about 15-20 meters from us stood an armed train guard. To this day, I do not know if he was German, Ukrainian or Lithuanian. He stopped and looked at us, and we looked at him for a moment that seemed like an eternity to us. We did not fear death—we had been living with it looming over our heads for several years—we were only afraid that we would be handed over to the Gestapo, since it meant terrible torture. We did not know what to do, for we could not go back, so Heniek said: "Let's go on ahead!" at that moment, when we moved, the guard turned his back to us and went in the opposite direction.

Several yards on, we found ourselves on the street, 100 meters from the entrance to the Hasag factory. There was a lot of movement there, as the shifts were changing. Only Polish and German workers could get in and out. There were people among them who knew us personally and looked at us with amazement: what were we, Jews, doing on the street and with a loaf of bread no less?

We later found out that one of the Polish workers reported seeing us to the Germans and after some time they began looking for us. Our foreman, Gunter, was convinced that we were hiding inside the factory and called us to give ourselves up, promising nothing would happen to us. The next day, when we were still missing from the morning census, they searched the barracks. After a few days, the Germans spread a rumor that we were caught and shot.

By that time, we were already on the Aryan side, on our way to Secemin. We had to pass through villages wearing the camp's clothes and the fact that we were foreigners could be seen from a distance. At first, we thought it was best to walk at night, but that proved impossible because we did not know the way and we were lost. We decided to walk during the day and sleep in the forest at night. The distance from Częstochowa to Secemin was about 50 kilometers, but the area was riddled with new lines of defense the Germans had prepared and German soldiers and their allies were lurking everywhere. We had to go in circles to avoid running into them.

If we met Poles along the way, we used to tell them that we ran away from a work camp in Germany and now we were going to join the partisans. As night was beginning to fall, we came across a farmer coming back from the field on his way home. After exchanging the Christian blessing "blessed be His glorious name forever," he asked us where we were from and where we were headed—he immediately noticed we were not from around those parts. We repeated our story and the farmer, upon hearing those words, invited us to his house for dinner. It turned out that he was one of the liaisons of the *National Military Forces* (NSZ)—Polish partisans from the radical right, who did not really fight the Nazis, but were canvassing the villages and forests for Jews and communists in order to kill them. By 1944, the number of volunteers joining these units had significantly dwindled.

During dinner, which the entire family attended, they talked about the war and about politics, but the main topic of conversation was their hatred of Jews and communists, especially novelist Wanda Wasilewska. We, ironically, had to agree with their views, maybe even more radically, so we would not be recognized as Jews. Luckily, we spoke very good Polish, without any accent. It was then decided that the next day, the famer would take us in his carriage to the National Army camp. After a rich dinner, he led us to the threshing floor, where we were supposed to stay the night. We did not sleep, for we had to escape within the next few hours. We waited until it was completely quiet and everyone was asleep and left the threshing floor quickly, heading in the opposite direction to which we were supposed to be taken the next day.

We had to reach a contact in the village, which was

not far from Secemin, someone that Lucek knew of: we were looking for a Pole named Roman Pindelak, whose cabin was at the edge of the village. Roman Pindelak helped partisans and Jews. He himself could not hide Jews at his house, for fear that the partisans would discover them. We safely reached Roman's house, where we were welcomed nicely, we were given dinner and slept in the cowshed.

The next day, Lucek led us to Secemin, to the threshing floor of Barbara Hajdas. We calculated the time so that we arrived to Barbara's at night, because we could be seen if we traveled by day and that would endanger not only us two, but all those that were staying with the Hajdas family. There was a group of young men hiding there, led by Bolek Gewercman, who was one of the older ones in the group. There were six people on the Hajdas family's threshing floor: the two Glixman brothers, as well as Bolek, Mecik, Jasik and Haim, who was a local man from Secemin and had brought the others there.

The group would spend most of its time sitting on the threshing floor, where an underground bunker had been dug, hidden from the outside so that no one could discover it. During the day, when everyone was sitting outside, one of the boys used to always stand guard. The cabin and the threshing floor both stood at the end of the village, very close to the edge of the forest. If there was any danger, everyone would quickly go down to the bunker. Barbara Hajdas would bring us food only under the cover of night, so that no one would notice. She would also clear the waste bucket. Bathing or cleaning of any kind was out of the question. We were infested with lice and it stung us constantly.

There were two guns and a pistol inside the bunker. Bolek always carried one gun in his belt and after two or three days of our stay on the threshing floor, he decided that since Lucek was in their group before us, he would get to stay and we had to leave, since there was not enough room for any more people. Heniek and I said that if we had to leave—so be it, but where would we go? Lucek stepped in and said decisively, "If they go, I'll go with them!" the group started arguing. There were those who opposed Bolek's decision, because they claimed—and rightly so—that he was sending us to a certain death. Barbara Hajdas, who was very respected within her family, was an interesting woman: she and her daughter, Tulka, demanded that we be allowed to stay. In light of all of that, Bolek backed down and we stayed.

After about two or three weeks into our stay on Mrs. Hajdas' threshing floor, Michael Deres, who was there once before, and Noladk, with whom Michael escaped from Hasag, arrived as well.

Life was completely different on Barbara's threshing floor. In Hasag, we were closed indoors and sleeping in barracks, side by side, with no privacy. We were working 12-hours a day, hard labor that demanded

The Hajdas family. On the right is Barbara, Righteous Among the Nations.

On the left: Tulka, Barbara's daughter, our liaison.

great precision and everything we did was supervised. Things were different at the Hajdas residence: first of all, we were no longer prisoners and we were no longer living under constant terror. We were not as hungry as we were in the camp and we were not working. The biggest problem was the fear, enormous tension and anxiety that one of the neighbors or the landlords' relatives would realize that something unusual was going on in the Hajdas residence and would report it to the Germans.

Barbara Hajdas, her daughter, and her family demonstrated great courage and altruism. These people took us in without any pay, since we did not have any material possessions. At that time, we were not receiving any financial aid from Antek, Isaac Zuckerman, from Warsaw or from the Jewish Combat Organization. Not only did we not have any money, the Hajdas family did not have the resources to buy basic food supplies for such a large group of people. I remember how we would go out at night armed with our entire arsenal of two guns and a pistol to rob nearby German farms. We took the food we needed to survive by force. These adventures were very dangerous, because we had to carry the goods on our shoulders and we were afraid someone would notice us. But these trips enabled us to survive through very hard times. The danger the Hajdas family faced was immense—to hide 12 young men—Jews no less! Other families eventually agreed to hide a few Jews, after they were persuaded to do so by Mrs. Hajdas.

It was time for the members of the group to go their separate ways. I was with Tadek, Mrs. Hajdas' son and there were two other men with me: the village leader, Icchak Ufner, and Jacob. The former was a revisionist in his ideological-political views, and the latter was a communist.

The conditions at Tadek's were very difficult. The bunker was a hole that was dug in the ground, it was 120 centimeter high, and two meters wide, so we could only sit or lie down on the hay. The hole was covered with wooden boards with hay on top of them, so what was underneath could not be seen. Near the opening, between the boards, there was an opening through which we were given food and our waste bucket would be taken out. On the sidewall of the bunker, there was a small opening through which air would enter. This entire structure was very well disguised.

We sat in this "tomb" for eight months. We were like prisoners in this hole because Tadek's cabin stood in the middle of Secemin village and there was no way we could come out, not even to the threshing floor. It was always dark inside and we did not know whether it was day or night outside. The bucket smelled. We could not even stretch our bones—all we could do was sit or lie down. I used a cup that was in my possession to brush my teeth: I would take some water into my mouth, wash my mouth with them and then spit them into my hands and use them to wash my face a little.

Those were horrible months that I will never forget.

The time we stayed there lasted forever. We could not even read, we had to be patient and it took a lot of willpower and physical stamina to get through this ordeal, with my two neighbors, between whom I was sleeping, having vehement political debates that would almost come to physical blows. I, who was the youngest of the bunch, had to separate and appease them.

We had nothing left to do. All of our conversations were conducted in whispers, so that no one would hear us or pay any attention to us. In that sense, we were all very disciplined; we knew what was expecting us if we were discovered. It is important, however, to note that we did not starve. We did not know who was bringing us food, because it was always in the evening, so the neighbors would not notice and it was dark inside and outside. Sometimes I was sick of it all, but it never crossed my mind to leave that hole.

It was 1944, and both fronts, the eastern and western, were moving: the former was moving east, and the latter—to the west. The German armies suffered great losses and were retreating, or as they put it, "took new positions," so we knew it was only a matter of time until the war would be over and we would be free. When we were sitting like that—lying in that grave, to be exact—I remembered my childhood, my mother, my father; bright and pleasant moments in my life, which gave me strength to go on.

When I moved to Tadek's, my brother Heniek,

Antek Zuckerman.

Michael Deres, and Nudelk went to stay with Jan Czapla, who lived in the Psary, a village three kilometers from Secemin. As Heniek told us later, the conditions there were better than ours because from time to time, it was possible to leave the bunker for the threshing floor and come out for some fresh air. Czapla had a different problem: his wife was afraid to hide Jews, but Jan was a determined man and the three Jewish boys were allowed to stay.

During that time, we reestablished contact with Antek Zuckerman from the Jewish Combat Organization in Warsaw. Antek was able to help and we began receiving money once again. Even though Warsaw was in ruins after the uprising in August 1944, Antek had an apartment there and Tulka, Barbara Hajdas' daughter, who was now the mother of a baby boy, served as our liaison to Antek. Riding the train in those times was very dangerous, as the Germans would sometimes raid them as well, taking young people off them for labor in Germany. That is why Tulka used to take her baby with her on those rides—the Germans would not take a mother from a baby. The baby, in diapers, protected his mother. Our situation began improving at that time and we could pay a little money to the people who were sheltering us.

We also wanted to help the Jews that were still in the Hasag camp and send them some money. My brother Heniek had a Polish friend he went to school with before the war, who he had accidently met when we were still in Hasag. The friend was still working in the factory then, so we knew his address and Tulka assumed a new and dangerous mission: she went to his house and asked if he would agree to transfer money to the Jews in Hasag. He agreed, and Tulka would go to his house every now and then and the money would get to Hasag.

December 1944. We did not know the war was about to end. At our request, Antek sent a Jewish doctor to examine us, because some of us were unwell, including me—I was suffering from a chronic cough. This doctor risked her life to get to us. She was a guest at the Hajdas residence and at night, we went with Jacob from Tadek's house to the Hajdas house to be examined. The winter of 1944 was very hard, and the frost and snow were very heavy.

On January 10, 1945, the Russian military forces standing on the banks of the Wisła River launched a massive attack. After a few days, we could hear the faint sounds of Russian artillery from our bunker. We then knew that the end to our terrible suffering was approaching and liberation was near.

I will never forget that day! It was January 17, 1945. Suddenly, the lid was pulled off our bunker. We saw daylight and Tadek's head. "Come out boys!" he yelled, "The Russians are in the village!"

Finally, we climbed out into the daylight. Our first act was to go to the Hajdas residence. We kept hearing various weapon shots along the way, Katyushas and automatic weapons. Battles were waging between the Russians and the Germans. The front line was moving.

We all assembled at Mrs. Barbara Hajdas' house. Jewish officers from the Soviet army advised us to leave as soon as possible and move east. They were concerned by a German counterattack, in which the Germans would temporarily reclaim those areas and murder us all; so our entire group went east. The road was completely empty, with only the occasional Russian military car passing by. At one point, a military jeep carrying a general stopped by and the general said: "And you, where are you going? You are in the middle of the front line!" The noise around us, the sound of fire, was awful and we, 14 boys, were walking in the midst of it all. Not one living soul was around us. In the evening, we arrived in a village.

The group divided between the village's cottages, together with the Soviet soldiers. There were two Soviet officers and their servant, a very young boy, in the house where I stayed. When the landlady asked us how many potatoes she should cook, one of them told her to ask the servant, because he was the youngest and ate the most. Bread was scarce then and potatoes were the most basic food. While they were waiting for dinner, the officers sang Arias from Russian operas. To their amazement, I named the operas the Arias were taken from. Surprised, they asked how I knew them, since in their minds, the Poles did not understand a thing—they were ignorant people.

The certificate of honor recognizing Barbara
Hajdas as Righteous Among the Nations.

The next day, I saw the Russians taking some German soldiers from one of the villages and shooting them with a Papasha, a Russian automatic rifle.

After some time had passed, we returned to Secemin. The military commander in Secemin was an officer with the Soviet army and as we later learned, he was a Jew. Two of us, who knew Yiddish, approached him and requested some food. He gave us a few bags of potatoes, but asked us not to tell anyone he was Jewish.

Some of us, like Bolek and others, returned to Częstochowa, but the majority stayed in Secemin. Jews who escaped from the camps started to appear, coming out of different hideouts. They were passing through Secemin on their way to the east. Lucek and I used to sit for days, peeling potatoes and cooking soup, to feed these hungry nomads.

We would occasionally visit the Hajdas family. Once, when I was there, a Russian military company came and set up a cantonment in the area. In such company, there was a *politruk*, a high-ranking officer, who would read the newspaper to the soldiers after their meals, explaining the situation on the front line.

I would sit on the side, listening, and then I would explain the situation on the front line to the soldiers in Russian and better than the politruk. To those who wondered, I explained that I acquired my knowledge at a Polish school.

Me on the right, and my brother Heniek on the left.

After a while, we returned to Częstochowa. Some among the group went on their way, while others stayed. We were staying in our apartment, as was a group of Jews who also survived. We had to find means to survive. I used to buy candles in Częstochowa and carry them in a backpack to the ruined city of Warsaw, where I stayed with Kazik Rathajzer's father. These trips were not easy because the trains were completely full and the ride would take a very long time.

"Aliyah Bet," the illegal immigration to Palestine began. Antek Zuckerman participated in this brave initiative. This immigration saw groups leave for Romania, and Heniek and I decided to leave Poland, which had become a big cemetery to us both. We were also influenced by certain Polish statements suggesting that while Hitler was terrible to the Poles, he did do something good for Poland—he cleansed it of Jews.

Not everyone in our group wanted to go. Some had left-wing views and they wanted to help rebuild a new Communist Poland. The Polish authorities knew us and threatened that if we did not work for the *Defense Ministry* (UB), we would be drafted into the army.

Bolek and some of the other men organized a group and left for Palestine, but he did not want to take Heniek and me with them. He wanted to get rid of us, so we would not tell anyone how he tried to kick us out of the Hajdas' bunker in Secemin. This demand meant a death sentence for us.

Everyone left and we remained in Częstochowa, but we wanted to get to Palestine, so we started looking for contacts that could help us. We knew where Antek was living, so we went to him and told him everything. He promised us that when the group would organize for departure, he would let us know when and where to go. And indeed, one day, at the end of February 1945, news had arrived that we were to report to a certain address in Krakow.

On March 8, 1945, we left Częstochowa for Krakow. There were a few young men already there, Jews from different parts of Poland and Lithuania. We stayed there for a few days. Several Russian inspections took place, but the landlady told them we were Greek Jews returning home. We had documents from the Russian, American, and British authorities and even from the International Red Cross, confirming that we were Greek Jews. The papers were false of course, but they were issued in different languages and they had multiple stamps on them. We had no problems crossing the border after presenting these documents.

Another period in our lives had come to its end. A new chapter, full of new question marks, had begun. The destination was clear: Palestine! But when will we get to the Jewish homeland we dreamed of so much? What will happen on the way? I left Poland with mixed emotions. My memories of my happy childhood among family and friends were mingled with the memories of the torture I endured during the Nazi occupation of Poland. Just as I never forgot what was good and beautiful in my young life, I never forgot the despair felt by men and women, young and old, during the days of the final liquidation of the ghetto in Częstochowa, my birthplace. The voices of the condemned transported to the death camps called to us: Jews, revenge! Revenge! Avenge our deaths!

I often wondered how I could heed their call. Have I truly done so?

My Revenge

It was the spring of 1945. We were still on our way and the war was still raging. Fierce battles were fought on all fronts. As I mentioned before, on March 8, 1945, Heniek and I traveled from Częstochowa to Krakow to join a group of Jews who were about to illegally cross many borders en route to Palestine, which was still under the British Mandate at the time. Our group consisted of twenty young people—the eldest among us was 25-years-old. Russian policemen and soldiers guarded the borders, with aim of catching Nazi criminals, who were trying to escape however they could. We were traveling with false papers, as Greek Jews returning to Greece from the Nazi concentration camps.

We were driving through Czechoslovakia and Hungary to Romania. I remember seeing a young Jewish man in traditional clothes at a little Hungarian train station, with a skullcap and sideburns on his head. I got out of the car and addressed him in Yiddish. He understood I was a Jew, but he could not answer because he did not know Yiddish and I did not speak Hungarian. To me it was incomprehensible because all the religious people in Poland spoke Yiddish, and almost no one spoke Polish.

We had quite a few language problems on the way. No one in the group spoke Greek. But there were a few from Lithuania and eastern Poland who had gone to Jewish schools before the war, and they spoke Hebrew. Since Hebrew was not a familiar language, it could pass as Greek to strangers. The rest of the group members did not open their mouths in public. We had to be very careful all the time because there were spies everywhere, including Soviet Jews, who could hand us over to the Soviet authorities.

This was how we reached Transylvania, where we stopped for a few days, heading to the resort town of Hunedoara. We saw quite a few Jews there, including elderly people and children. We were moved by it, since we had not seen any children or elderly people since 1942. We came to Hunedoara, where a kibbutz of sorts was being organized. They needed money, a lot of money, because living expenses and other services had to be paid for; and we, who just came out of concentration camps, forests and bunkers, were penniless. We soon found out that various Jewish-American charities in Romania were donating money to sustain us. These organizations were banned in Poland. Organizations such as ours, a makeshift kibbutz, were being put together in other places as well, including Bucharest.

Conditions in Romania were good. We had plenty of food and other essential items. There was a small Jewish community in Hunedoara that treated us very well. Our group comprised mainly of young men and the local Jews hooked us up with their daughters. After about two months, we packed our bags again and continued on our journey south, closer to Italy. On the Yugoslavian border, the Serbs became intrigued by us, thinking we were Nazi fugitives. One of the women in our group was wearing trousers and it seemed suspicious to them. They sent an officer to investigate us. He turned out to be an intelligent young man. My brother Heniek tried to explain who we were—we could not tell him the truth, of course, but he explained to him that we were Greek Jews returning to Greece after difficult experiences in the Nazi camps. The officer accepted our explanations and allowed us continue on our way to Belgrade. There, like everywhere else, they were ready for us.

We were walking down a street one day, speaking in Polish, when we met some people from the Polish embassy. They were very happy to see us, because they thought we were from the Polish delegation that had come for the communist youth convention in Belgrade. We did not deny it, but we got out of there right away. You have to keep in mind that we were in a country with a pro-Soviet government and if we were identified for who we really were; we would have found ourselves on our way to Siberia instead of Palestine.

After several days, we left for Zagreb by train and headed to the Trieste Port in Italy. We were nervous when we approached the Italian border: we were going to a free country and there was a meticulous inspection waiting for us at the border. But we passed it successfully and reached Trieste. The train was traveling along to the coastline and for the first time in my life, I saw the ocean. The impression it made on me was enormous. Heniek and I stood up and watched it through the train window. We could not get enough of the sight.

When we reached Trieste, we asked in English for the address of the place where we had to go. Until that time, we spoke only German. In Trieste, we felt safe. When our group went up on the tram, the ticket collector came to us and demanded that we buy tickets. We told him we were refugees and that we had no money. There was a British officer on that train and without a word, he walked up to the ticket collector and paid for our tickets. And so, after many adventures, we reached the collection point.

After several days, we left for Udine where a unit of the Jewish brigade from Palestine was stationed. Italy was the gathering point for all the European Jews who survived the war, mostly young people. From the moment we arrived, we were under the supervision of the brigade soldiers. In Italy, I felt more than anything that when I told an Italian that I was a Jew, he accepted it very naturally and did not react with amazement or reluctance. I felt that to him, I was an equal among equals.

Our group was taken from Udine to Modena, where a large number of refugees had already gathered. We stayed in a large building that once serves as a military academy. This large number of refugees from all over Europe was under the care of UNRRA, the United Nations Relief and Rehabilitation Administration.

Various political alliances were formed among the different refugees, Zionists and others. A group from Vilna, our group from Koniecpol, and others formed an organization called "Revenge." My brother Heniek was a member. The goal was to get to France, because it was closer to Germany. One of the leaders of the group was Aba Kobner. At that time, Heniek went to Paris and I joined *Hashomer Hatzair* (The Youth Guard) movement that left Modena for Rome.

An apartment in the labor district of Lungotevere was rented for us in Rome. The conditions were difficult: It was very hot in Italy in June and we were not used to such a climate. We could not sleep in the suffocating apartment and many of us slept on the roof. I remember that not far from there, in the little piazzas, were cafés where entire families would meet. They brought food with them, whatever they had, ordered something to drink in the café and just sat there. Others brought different musical instruments and spent the evenings playing games and singing Italian songs. The latest hit was "Mama Son Tanto Felice."

We were waiting to be transferred to Ostia-Lido di Roma, where conditions were much better. Since we did not have anything to do and I was the master of my own time, I toured Rome and the Vatican with some

A document I received from the Polish consul in Rome,
which served as an ID card, 1945.

Me, and some friends in Italy, waiting to immigrate to Israel, 1945.

friends. In the meantime, I found out that every Sunday before noon Pope Pius XII was giving an audience. One Sunday, I organized a group of my friends and we went to the Vatican. Before we entered the hall, we had to announce who we were, where we came from, etc. I was the official group representative. I spoke German to the priest. He asked me different questions, and was mostly interested in whether we were communists from Poland. He was probably worried we would interrupt the audience. I explained that we were Jews, and that we had nothing to do with communism—that was why we left Poland.

They let us enter an enormous, elegant hall full of people who were waiting for the Pope as well. After a while, surrounded by an entourage of people from Switzerland and their companions, the Pope was carried in on his throne. All the attendants, except for us, who were standing in the corner, knelt. The Pope looked at our direction and smiled a little, he probably understood who we were. He made a short speech, bestowed a blessing on everyone, and after a while the short address ended. One day, when I was touring the Sistine Chapel at the Vatican, I met a group of Polish soldiers. I sat behind them to hear the fascinating explanations of the tour guide.

After a while, we moved from Rome to Ostia-Lido di Roma, on the coastline, not far from Rome. We were given a beautiful house that once belonged to some fascist nobleman. There were no beds or furniture only matrasses on the floor, but there were sheets, pillows and blankets, which were luxuries for us. There was a joint dining room and a kitchen, like in a kibbutz, and we relied on UNRRA for all of our living expenses. Since we had no work, UNRRA representatives brought us sewing machines. There were many girls in our group and they sewed shirts and other clothes for UNRRA. At that time, I was writing my memoirs about my experiences in Poland during the Nazi occupation.

Every now and then, I traveled to Milan, where the European refugee center was located. The center received money and allocated it to the different kibbutzim, and I was sent to bring it. I went dressed as an American soldier because the Allied soldiers did not pay for train tickets. The journey lasted several hours in each direction. I was among locals, I did not speak Italian—I only knew a few expressions—but somehow, they could always guess what I wanted. They always offered me some supplies for the road from whatever they had taken with them, and I did not turn down the gesture. At that time, Soviet Russia was very popular. I knew Russian songs, mostly partisan songs, so I sang to them, evoking great enthusiasm. Everyone was happy. When I ran out of Russian songs, we would sing Italian songs together. I brought money for our kibbutz from my journeys to Milan. I would also use that opportunity to walk around the city. I was mostly taken aback by the cathedral.

At that time, Ostia was plagued by great poverty. I remember that when we would finish our meals and had leftovers, Italian children with little pots would come to the gate and our girls, who were working in the kitchen, would take food out to them.

In the summer, we passed our time at the beach. The girls in our group had more things to do: they cooked, sewed, and cleaned. Spirits were high. From time to time, Jewish brigade soldiers would visit us, telling us stories about Israel, and we would tell them about our experiences. There were other kibbutzim that were established in Ostia back then.

Everyone was waiting for a sign to continue on the journey. I spent six months in Ostia and during this entire time, small ships carrying refugees accompanied by Jews from Palestine were sailing in. On December 1945, we were told that we had to choose 25 candidates, men and women, to immigrate to Israel. Our leaders were seeing how more and more people were coming to Italy and decided to rent bigger ships that could carry a larger number of passengers. Our group found itself in that first big sail.

A big truck with Jewish soldiers appeared one day, we got inside, and it started driving toward a small port in the town of La Spezia, south of Genoa. The truck was covered with canvas, so that no one could see what was inside it and we had to sit very still. The plan was that two trucks from different parts of Italy would arrive in La Spezia at night and we had to be vigilant, because the British made it very difficult for Jews to immigrate to Palestine. The Italian policemen on the platforms were on our side. They did not like the British, so they cooperated with us.

We sailed on a ship named the *Enzo Sireni*, which was converted from a cargo ship into a unique passenger ship. Fabric hammocks were hung underneath its deck, so the passengers were hanging one over the other, only several centimeters apart. The entire ship was full of hammocks with people in them. There were only two bathrooms. It was dirty, stifling, and crowded and we felt ill, but unlike life in the camp, where we did not know when or even if we were going to come out alive, here I knew that the journey will end.

One of the hardest things about this journey was the thirst. We received a glass of water per day and we were given very little food because of the uncertainty concerning exactly how long this journey would take, and how long we would have to remain at sea. The water barrels were guarded so that no one could get to them. We spent most of the time on the deck, because conditions down below were unbearable. Fortunately, the cruise was in December and it was not hot.

When a ship would appear on the horizon, everyone had to descend below deck—the ship could not be seen as carrying passengers. We sailed like that for 10-12 days. One day, when we were probably pretty close to shore, a British airplane appeared, circled in the sky above us and then flew away. After several hours, two

British battle ships arrived and our captain was ordered to sail between them. The captain was Italian, but there were also some boys from the Palyam, the naval force of the Palmach on board, as well as a commander, a radioman and others, who during this entire time were in contact with Haifa. Once we were intercepted by the British, the restrictions on food and water in the ship were removed—there was no need to conserve them since our journey was about to be over. Finally, we could drink as much water as we wanted and eat until we were satiated.

On the first or second day of January 1946, our ship docked in Haifa. We stayed aboard the ship for several days, carefully guarded by British and Arab policemen. We assumed that the Jewish Agency and the British were holding negotiations over what to do with us.

After a few days, buses and many British policemen and soldiers appeared. We came ashore using a ladder and were met by the British, who counted us carefully. There were crates with oranges on the pier at that time, packed and ready for shipment to Europe. Jewish workers were packing the boxes—they were forbidden to come close to us, but they found a way to express themselves: they opened the crates and threw oranges at us.

People were told to board buses directly from the ship. We were taken, under police escort, to a camp in the city of Atlit. At that time, the Hebrew newspapers did not know how many Jews were on board the *Enzo*

Sireni and they wrote that it carried about 300-400 passengers. Their astonishment knew no limits: how could so many people be crammed into such a small ship?

The British arrested the captain, but before he disembarked, he gave us a little speech in French, which was very moving. We bid him farewell with applause and hoorays. Several Italian sailors from the crew mingled and disembarked with us and we all driven to Atlit. After a short while, the Jewish Agency quietly removed them from our camp and they were allowed to go back to Italy.

The conditions in Atlit were bearable. We stayed in barracks and had beds, pillows and blankets. The Jewish Agency was running the kitchen and the food was good. During our stay in Atlit, the British secret police, which had Jewish officers as well, interrogated us. They wanted to know how we arrived in Italy, where we were beforehand, how we left Italy, what route we sailed on, etc. We were ready for these interrogations: the people from the Jewish Agency told us not to say anything and just give them our first and last names and age, and insist that we were Jews from Israel—and that was what we did.

After a month, buses came and asked us where we wanted to go. Those who had family or acquaintances they could stay with were taken to their desired location. We, who were essentially homeless, were taken to Kfar Masaryk, a kibbutz affiliated with Hashomer Hatzair.

Me, second on the left, with some friends in Kibbutz Kfar Masaryk, 1946.

Me, on the right, with friends in Kibbutz Kfar Masaryk, 1946.

The kibbutz offered us a cold and unpleasant welcome. We lived in tents and slept in beds that were given to us by the Jewish Agency. We were always assigned the most difficult jobs. Several families who came from Poland treated us amicably, but the rest were indifferent to us. I worked very hard on the kibbutz, but if I asked for something, I never got it. In fact, we were treated as a mere workforce. I also started learning Hebrew on the kibbutz.

In May 1946, my brother Heniek came to Israel, also illegally, and spent some time in the Atlit camp. After he left Atlit, his group joined Ein HaHoresh, another Hashomer Hatsair kibbutz. Heniek did not join them and since he had nowhere to go, he slept on a bench on Rothschild Avenue in Tel Aviv. After a short while, the Jewish Agency sent him to Zair Avni, who gave him a place to stay for free.

I left the kibbutz in October 1946. Heniek and I rented a room in Bnei Brak. It was a small room in the yard, a cell with a small window, really. The property owner demanded that we give her six months-rent in advance, but my brother and I did not have money, so we decided to write to New York, to our only aunt, our mother's sister, asking for help. She immediately sent us $200, which was a fortune in those days. We were three people living in that cell, my brother and I and another friend from Częstochowa. In the summer, the room was stifling. The bathroom was outside. We did not even have a refrigerator, which was considered a luxury item back then, so we put the margarine in water to prevent it from melting. We cooked on a primus stove. Heniek started working as a locksmith in a British factory called Shopim. He was paid a minimal sum, and ate lunch there. I was working in government initiative jobs several days a month. I told the Histadrut I had to get a job because I did not have money to buy bread and they said, "If you don't have anything to eat, go to a kibbutz."

I wrote my uncle in New York and told him that I could not get a job. My uncle then wrote to an acquaintance of his in the field of stone work—Melinsorf, the gravestone manufacturer, who he had met in Poland before the war—and that was how I got a job making gravestones, earning 80 piestres, while the others got £1.

The attitude toward us was not friendly. People had no idea what we went through and they did not care. They mocked us, saying we went like sheep to slaughter, that we did not fight the Germans. I realized I had no one to talk to and I withdrew into myself. This attitude lasted until 1961, the year they found Adolf Eichmann in Argentina and brought him to Israel. Eichmann's trial was aired on the radio and reported in the newspapers. There were many Holocaust survivors who testified in the trial, telling the court where they were and what they had endured. I remember how people were standing in the streets, listening very attentively to these testimonies. They finally started to understand what we went through.

Heniek had wanted to be an engineer since he was a child and he decided to try to make his dream come true. We went to Haifa together, to apply to the Israel Institute of Technology, so he could realize his dream. When the secretary, who was elegantly dressed, heard about Heniek's wish to enroll, he asked him, "What do you want to study here for? There is no industry here and you won't even have a job. It's better that you study construction." But Heniek insisted and got accepted.

Acts of resistance against the British Mandate continued all that time. The British declared a curfew, there were raids, and those were uneasy times. In the summer of 1947, we moved to Haifa so Heniek could study at the Technion. We did not know anyone there, but Mr. Avni, with whom my brother stayed back in the day, had an acquaintance in Haifa, Ziuma Zarhi, so we had at least one address to call on. After using many connections, I got a job in the British Bureau for Public Jobs as the apprentice to a Jewish plumber. I did not work very hard, but I did not earn much money, either; and so Heniek was studying and I was working.

On April 2, 1947, the British Mandate over Palestine ended and after prolonged discussion, the United Nations set a vote on the territory for November 29, 1947. The historic vote saw 13 countries vote against and 33 countries vote in favor of revoking the British Mandate and splitting Palestine into two countries,

Jewish and Arab. The next day, the Arab militaries attacked and since Haifa was home to a mixed population, violent clashes persisted day and night. At night, I would lie in my bed and hear the echoes of those battles and I would think to myself, that there I was, while our people were fighting and risking their lives. It bothered me.

At the beginning of 1948, I was recruited as a volunteer in the Haganah and joined the units assigned to protect the Jewish neighborhoods in Haifa. I was stationed in the old city center. I was given a Parabellum gun, munitions, and two grenades—that was my entire arsenal. It is important to point out that we feared the British more than the Arabs. The British would sentence to death any Jew found to be in the possession of a gun. After a while, the Haganah also recruited all of the students at the Technion, including my brother Heniek. It was April 1948. We had no uniforms and everyone wore their own clothes. At that time, the Haganah headquarters decided to conquer Haifa and rid the city of enemies. My brother and I participated in those battles: my brother was in the force that came down the Carmel on Stenton Street and I was on the force that went up that same street. The Arab population, seeing what was going on, fled.

Me, on the right, during the liberation of Haifa, April 1948.

On May 15, 1948, the British had to leave the country. A short while before that I was officially drafted to the Carmeli Unit in Battalion 24.

With the British retreat and the Declaration of Independence, we were attacked by all the neighboring Arab countries, including the armies of Iraq. The War of Independence had begun. Our unit was transferred to the upper Galilee, where we participated in many battles. On October 22, 1948, we were sent to open the route to Kibbutz Manara.

I suffered a leg wound in the battle. I bandaged my leg as best as I could and started rolling toward the road, where ambulances were picking up the wounded. They took me as well. It turned out that I was hit by an anti-armor bullet despite the fact I was sitting in an armored vehicle. I was hospitalized for a week in a field hospital in Kfar Giladi and was later transferred in an ambulance to the military hospital in Haifa. The bullet severed the main nerve in my leg and I had to undergo several surgeries, but despite everything, my left leg remained paralyzed.

When I was lying in the hospital, Mina Yosefberg, who I met in March 1948, before Haifa was liberated, nursed me. She would bring me sandwiches and most importantly, since I was forbidden to get up, she brought me books to read. Due to different complications resulting from the surgeries, I only left the hospital in May 1950. I found myself on the street and since I

The War of Independence. Me, as a soldier in Carmeli Unit,
Battalion 24, Company A.

had nowhere to go, I went to Bat Galim, to a shelter for the homeless, such as me.

Heniek was still in the army at that time. We started looking for an apartment, which proved to be a difficult task since there were simply no apartments to rent.

I had a hard time walking around and had to use crutches. Heniek found a place for us on Abbes Street and after some much-needed renovation, it was living-ready. He went to the office that was handling the property, but no one was willing to speak with him. The office was on the second floor and I remember how hard it was for me to climb up there on crutches. When they saw Heniek and me, their attitude changed completely, because I had demanded—not asked—their attention. Eventually, they rented us the place, under the condition that we will renovate it at our own expense and they would take it out of our rent money.

We borrowed the money for the renovation from Mina Yosefberg and Ziuma Zarhi. We moved in and Heniek returned to school. His girlfriend Shulamit, who later became his wife, was a social worker. I was recognized as a disabled war veteran. The Defense Ministry took care of disabled veterans and promoted an initiative to form a taxi cooperative, of which I became a member. We received our paycheck whether we worked or not, but after several months we decided to dismantle the cooperative, since its expenses were greater than its incomes. Each one of us received half of a taxi license number. I worked 12-14 hours a day, on Saturdays and

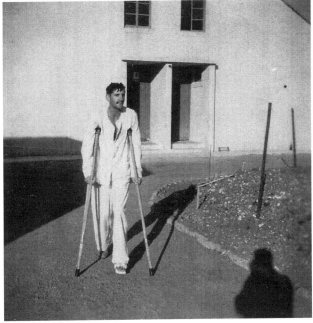

Me, after I was injured on October 22, 1948,
in a battle on the way to Manara.

holidays too, and after a while, I was able to buy my partner's half of the license.

Meanwhile, Heniek married Shulamit and she came to live with us. The young couple lived in the bedroom and I moved into the small kitchen. I was working my fingers to the bone, as they say, and saving every penny I could until I had enough money to buy a small apartment near Haifa. I left the apartment on Abbes Street to Heniek.

With time, I realized that driving a cab was not the profession for me. In 1961, I sold my cab, I had some savings, and I bought a 25 percent stake in a gas station in Ramat Gan. I sold the apartment and bought a ground-level apartment in Ramat Gan. My savings were not enough, so I borrowed some money from my brother and some friends. The apartment was somewhat far from the gas station and I did not have money for lunch or for the bus. I had to use everything I earned to pay back the money I borrowed. I paid my brother back as well, to the very last penny. After years of saving, I bought a new one-and-a-half bedroom apartment in Ramat Gan, closer to my job.

In 1978, I met Irena, who also survived the Holocaust as a child. We got married and are still happily married to this very day. Sometime after we married, we wanted to move away from the hustle and bustle of Tel Aviv. During our quest, we reached Ariel. The town suited us in every way, so we bought a small semi-detached house there.

In the early 1990s, when Irena stopped working, we moved to Ariel. In Ariel, my wife took up some community work in a local culture center. From our interaction with the city's youth, we saw that they knew very little about the Holocaust, even though there were those who participated in school trips to Poland and saw the Nazi death camps. We had no idea there was such ignorance on the subject of the Holocaust, since we did not have children of our own. We, who have lived through the hell of that extermination, were stunned. It turned out that it was not only the youth who knew so little—the adults did not know much about what happened to the Jews in Europe during World War II, either.

We decided to do something. It started with me telling young people, who came to our house, about what had happened to the Jews in Europe under the Nazi occupation. In order to expand our activities, we asked the manager of the cultural center, Mrs. Esther Dagan, to allocate some space for us to that effect. She gave us two walls on which we hung pictures and other items related to the Holocaust. Little by little, schools started to show some interest in our work and classes would come to visit the little exhibition, especially ahead of Holocaust Remembrance Day.

We decided to expand our activities, and to that end, we bought a big private home in Ariel, which we renovated and expanded according to our needs.

Irena's Story

I was born in January 1936 to Sophie and Moshe Zimmermann. My parents came from a city called Przemyśl. They were born to poor families, and went out to seek a better life in the salt mines of Zakopane, near Krakow. My parents met and married in the city. When the war broke out, I was three and a half years old, so I do not remember much of those days. Most of what I know about my childhood I was told when I was older, but slivers of memories remained with me.

My first memory is from the first day of the war. My mother took me to the rear balcony, pointed to the red sky, and said, "Look, the war has started!" I looked at the horizon and saw a big fire and many flashes of light. The next day everyone understood that it was a world war.

My father was soon drafted into the Polish army. After a while, he returned and took my mother and me to his place of birth, Przemyśl. There was already a ghetto there and we went to live in my grandmother's house, my father's mother, together with some of my other uncles.

One day, my mother left the house and did not come

back. She had disappeared. With time, I learned that the Germans held a raid that day, apprehending Jews and sending them to the camps. To this day, I do not have any information about her fate.

There is another event that is etched in my mind: I was sitting on the windowsill, looking on the streets of the ghetto underneath me, when I saw a group of women and children led by soldiers. Suddenly, someone lifted me up from my place, gave me a decent spank, and said, "You shouldn't be here!" At that time there were rumors going around that the ghetto was about to be liquidated.

A gentile woman, who was an old friend of my father's, came to my grandmother's house one day. He had asked her to take care of me and she managed to smuggle me out of the ghetto. She wanted to take my aunt Ada too, but Ada did not go because she wanted to stay and live with her mother. Thanks to that act, my life was saved.

I have another memory of escaping that ghetto. It was a particularly dark night and I was with a group of people who were crossing a river. I was sitting on someone's shoulders and the water reached his neck, so part of my body also was submerged in water. I held on to the man's hair so I would not fall. It was cold and I was very scared. I remember the sound of the water and being made to stay absolutely quiet. That was how we crossed the border.

My father's friend took me to her place of work on a

German's farm in Złoczów. One day, she asked me to go up to the warehouse above the stables and give someone food. I opened the door with a key I had and found a dark boy with curly black hair. I gave him the food and continued doing so every day: I would bring him food, play with him a little, and take out his waste bucket. I was disgusted with the smell and it was a difficult experience that made me sad and brought me to tears. That experience has left its mark on me to this day.

One day, I went up to see him as usual, but he was not there. I asked the gentile woman where he was and she said that he was taken away. With time, it turned out that the boy was tired of sitting in the closed room and ran away. A German soldier noticed him, realized he was a Jewish boy, pulled out his gun and shot him on the spot.

And another memory: I was walking with the gentile woman on the street, it was probably a Sunday. An old Polish woman came to us and said, "Who is this girl? Where is she from? You were never married or pregnant, so why do you have a child? She must be Jewish!" She went to the Gestapo and informed on us. Someone told the gentile woman about that and advised that she should organize the necessary papers before she was interrogated by the Gestapo.

The next day she drove to her childhood village and brought papers proving that she was not Jewish but a gentile. She also brought with her the birth certificate of a gentile girl who died bearing my name. And indeed, several days later we were called for questioning by the Gestapo. I wore a pretty dress, new shoes and had a nice ribbon in my hair. On the way, the woman taught me what to say if they ask me questions. I treated her as my own mother.

We entered a room and I saw people in uniform sitting next to a tall desk. I was told to stand in the middle of the room and turn around where I stood.

I passed the test!

If they had determined that I was Jewish, they would have killed me and my adoptive mother, as well as her entire family. The woman panicked, so she sent me to her mother, who was living in the forest with her husband, who was a ranger. She took pity on me and brought me somewhere else. I was transferred from place to place, mainly to places where there were more children.

Another memory: I arrived at a family who had a catering business for weddings. The woman used to make poppy cakes with raisins. After she was done, she would let me lick the bowl. I can still remember how they tasted and ever since then, I love poppy cakes.

One of the families served potatoes with some oil. Everyone grabbed as much as they could and we received milk, too. I went out with the animals to pasture, but my shoes were too big, so I filled them with paper. The clothes were oversized and worn out as well. When we went to church, I held my shoes in my hand while we were crossing the creek—I did not want to ruin them.

That was how the days of the war went by for me. I had no permanent home, nor did I have a mother or a father. I did not know what love and affection were.

The war was over in 1945. My father had survived and after a long search he found me and we were reunited. He started a new family and I was moved from one boarding school to the next. I studied chemistry in Poland and in 1957, I came to Israel and reached Kibbutz Gesher.

Home.

We made it. I, together with my wife who joined me wholeheartedly from the start, with enthusiasm, energy, skill and a sense of commitment to fulfilling my dream, we created a home.

Our Home—Ariel Holocaust and Heroism Memorial House

Our place was legally registered as a social organization.

What does our home look like?

We have spared no effort or expense to make sure that our home looks the part on the outside, as well. We purchased a big, six-story building on 44 Nachshonim Street in Ariel, which needed extensive renovations. The memorial center spans four floors and we use the two remaining floors as our private residence.

We collected the items for the exhibits over a long period of time, trying to get authentic pieces. We were able to obtain personal documents and effects. People interested in commemorating their loved ones, and spreading the word of the Holocaust, gave some items to us. We purchased many items from public auctions and from private individuals, as well, mainly in Poland.

When I saw the statues in Tel Aviv made by Samuel Willenberg, a Holocaust survivor from the Treblinka death camp, I could not calm down until we purchased some of the artist's most impressive works. He commemorated the Treblinka victims during the death shipments, as he remembered their last moments before they were murdered in the gas chambers or with a gunshot.

Each character had a unique story: Some we knew by their first and last names and what they said in their last moments. Like a girl from Warsaw, for example, who while her beautiful hair was being shorn, told Willenberg—who was shaving her head—that her name was Ruth Dorfman, that she was from Warsaw, that she did her matriculation exam and that she was 20-years-old. She also asked how long it took to die in the gas chambers and whether it was painful. Just after, she was murdered in the gas chambers.

One of the statues shown in our gallery is that of musicians in the camp orchestra, which was established by the SS. They were chosen from among the most renowned Jewish musicians in Europe, and sent to their deaths in the gas chambers. Among them was Artur Gold, a violinist and a composer, who wrote several famous pieces before World War II. The artist did not live long in Treblinka and was dead by 1942.

My wife, Irena, accompanies the guests who visit our center, presenting each one with one of the figures that were commemorated in bronze. That way, we try to make the famous motto "each Holocaust victim has a name" come true.

We show rare photographs in a gallery that chronologically represents each stage of the Holocaust. The gallery of personal effects exhibits prisoners' clothes, including the striped outfit left behind by a known Jewish-Polish prisoner at Auschwitz. Other items, such as prisoners' dishes, different kinds of personal possessions, insignias of official ranks, ancient prayer books found, a page ripped from the Torah and was purchased by Jews to prevent further sacrilege, are also on display.

There is also a gallery of postcards and stamps in the exhibition. I have been collecting stamps for years as a hobby, and I now have a rather extensive collection. Among others, there is a collection of stamps organized by topics and letters from the camps, from the ghettoes and from other correspondence related to the Holocaust years. I included this collection in the items on display at the memorial center. On our annual trips to Europe, we were able to purchase additional philatelic items, mainly in public auctions. We have a special affinity to this collection because every postcard or letter in it represents the fate of a person who was tortured in a camp or in a ghetto, and who shortly after writing the postcard or letter was murdered by the Nazis.

We show these collections with Hebrew translations and essential explanations. It took nearly three years to translate the content to Hebrew, with the volunteer work of high school students in Ariel.

A separate area dedicated to photographed materials and different forms of wartime advertising are shown in chronological order, from the time the German conqueror entered Poland, through to the escalating persecutions, and all the way to the final extermination.

Sometimes, after a visit in the center, people bring us personal souvenirs that they had kept at home from those years. Not long ago, we received a present from a woman in Poland who visited us. It was a two and a half meter long Torah scroll, with scorch marks, that someone apparently rescued from a burning synagogue. We are not sure where this Torah scroll came from, but we believe it was from the Łódź Ghetto.

After a visit to the top floors of the house, I lead the guests downstairs to a 100-seat lecture hall, equipped with an audiovisual system and a collection of books on the subject. After the guests take their places, I give a short lecture, whose content I choose according to the listeners. The crowds are diverse: sometimes they are older people, sometimes they are part of group visits by high school or university students, or groups of soldiers with their commanders. Yeshiva students visit us as well. We show films on the subject and encourage a discussion.

Our Holocaust memorial center was established in 2003. During the first two years the visits were scarce, but by 2005, we already had 2,000 visitors and in 2006—many more. Guests come not only from nearby areas, but also from all over the country. We also host youth groups before their trips to Poland. We try to tell the visitors about the destruction of the European Jewry, to tell them about the Holocaust, so this knowledge finds its way to their hearts and their minds.

Our home has also drawn the attention of several

Israeli heritage centers and we are occasionally featured in newspapers. Former President Moshe Katsav and his wife have visited us. A Polish television station filmed a movie about our center, which has since aired several times on Polish TV.

We are constantly trying to enrich our home with more documentary material. We are aware of the importance of our work, because as the years go by, the witnesses to the Holocaust become fewer in numbers and the public's interest grows weaker.

My wife Irena, who was saved as a child by escaping to the Aryan side, and I, cannot forget and cannot grow weak. The faces of those who were led to their deaths have not disappeared and will never disappear from my memory; nor will the memory of how they were calling to us, those who remained behind, to avenge their blood. Then, at that moment, I knew that if I survived, I would fulfill their wish.

Over the years, I asked myself why I had survived instead of millions of other Jews. I realized that others and I were left alive to tell their story, to testify to what really happened. They died anonymously and I, who survived, have immortalized them in the minds of generations to come.

When I sit in the lecture hall in our memorial center and look at the faces of the people who are listening to me, who follow the movie, riveted, asking questions, expressing their opinions, arguing, and wanting to know more; when I see so many young faces, I know I am fulfilling their wish. And I know that the experience those visiting the memorial center had, will stay with them as a personal experience.

This is my revenge on those who exterminated my people.

This is My Revenge!

"This child and so many others like him, the younger generations, is my REAL Revenge."
Yaakov "Kuba" Wodzislawski

The Gallery

Photos taken by Jews and Germans at different times during the war. They are a living testimony to the horrors of the Holocaust.

An armband. Jews in Poland were made to wear one on their right arm.

A yellow patch that Jews in Germany were forced to wear on their clothing.

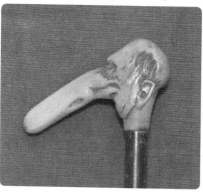

An ivory headpiece of a walking cane with distinct anti-Semitic overtones.

An original prisoner's jacket from the Auschwitz concentration camp which was worn by Mordechai Francoise, Jewish prisoner number 8721.

Mordechai, who was born in Poland, was imprisoned in the Łódź Ghetto.

His wife and daughter were sent to Chełmno extermination camp where they were murdered.

Mordechai was sent to Auschwitz in 1944 after the liquidation of the ghetto. He was able to save himself by escaping the "Death March."

He died in Poland in 1997.

The Lecture Hall

The hall hosts lectures on the Holocaust and its consequences. It is equipped with an audiovisual system. A library offering books on the subject is also available.

The Statue Gallery

The statues are the work of Samuel Willenberg, one of the revolutionaries that took part in the Treblinka uprising. After his escape from the concentration camp, he joined the Polish underground to fight against the Germans. He creates his art to give testimony to "the tragedy that was Treblinka."

A prisoner in the Treblinka extermination camp fighting in the mutiny.

A German Jew, a WWI hero, protested the harsh conditions in Treblinka. When he came to the camp, he demanded to see a doctor and was sent to the clinic, where he was killed by a shot to the head.

A father taking off his son's shoes, before entering the "showers"—
the gas chambers. The son is holding a shoelace in his hand.

A mentally ill girl holding on to her last treasure—bread.
She was shot dead at the clinic.